ROMANTIC STRATHSPEY

THE HEN WIFE. Portrait by Waitt of Maggie Sinclair

ROMANTIC STRATHSPEY

Its Lands, Clans and Legends

by

JAMES ALAN RENNIE

Illustrated

ROBERT HALE LIMITED
63 Old Brompton Road London S.W.7

First published 1956

PRINTED IN GREAT BRITAIN BY
NORTHUMBERLAND PRESS LIMITED
GATESHEAD ON TYNE

CONTENTS

APPENDIX

LIST OF ILLUSTRATIONS

ACKNOWLEDGMENTS

The illustrations nos. 10, 11, 12 and 21 are reproduced from photographs supplied by A. Ledingham.
The remaining illustrations are reproduced from
photographs taken by the author.

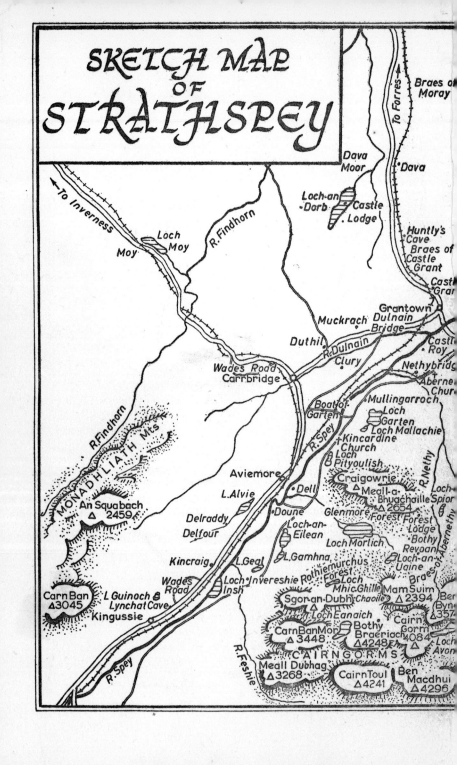

SKETCH MAP
OF
STRATHSPEY

To Forres

Braes of Moray

To Inverness

Dava Moor

Dava

Loch-an-Dorb

Castle Lodge

Huntly's Cave

Braes of Castle Grant

Castle Grant

Loch Moy

Moy

R.Findhorn

Grantown

Muckrach

Dulnain Bridge

Duthil

R.Dulnain

Clury

Castle Roy

Nethybridge

Aberne Chur

Wades Road
Carrbridge

Boat of Garten

Mullingarroch

Loch Garten

Loch Mallachie

R.Spey

R.Findhorn

MONADHLIATH Mts

Kincardine Church

Loch Pityoulish

Craigowrie

R.Nethy

Aviemore

L.Alvie

Dell

Meall-a-Bhuachaille 2654

Loch Spior

An Squabach 2459

Delraddy

Delfour

Doune

Glenmore Forest

Forest Lodge

Revoan Bothy

Loch-an-Eilean

Loch Morlich

Loch-an-Uaine

Braes of Abernethy

Kincraig

L.Geal

L.Gamhna

Rothiemurchus Forest

Loch Mhic.Ghille Chaoile

Mam Suim 2394

Ben Bynac 3574

Carn Ban 3045

Wades Road

Loch Invereshie

Loch Insch

Sgor-an-Dubh

Loch Eanaich

Cairn Gorm 4084

L Guinoch
Lynchat Cave

Kingussie

Carn Ban Mor 3448

Bothy Braeriach 4248

Loch Avon

CAIRNGORMS

R.Feshie

Meall Dubhag 3268

Cairn Toul 4241

Ben Macdhui 4296

R.Spey

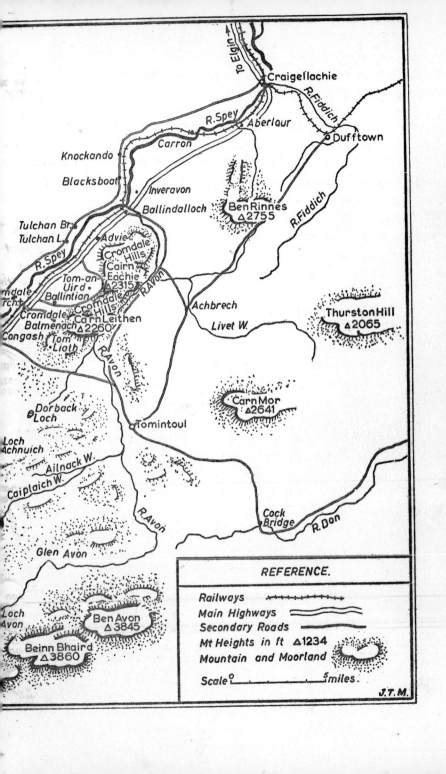

WHEN Robert Burns came to Strathspey in 1787 his muse was not in singing mood. The only record he has left us of his visit is a four-word entry in a note-book:

"Strathspey, rich and romantic."

For one who, like myself, lives in this magic land and finds in it "every joy of man's desiring", such brevity is disappointing, and yet it is preferable to the effusions of a later visitor who tells us that in Strathspey he found a land "reeking with romance".

That is not a happy turn of phrase. The verb "to reek" suggests restricted space and clogged atmosphere, and cannot, therefore, claim the remotest aptitude when applied to the fair and smiling strath of Spey. Even during the season of heather-burning the white smoke rising from the high hill-pastures mingles so quickly with the woolly clouds of the heavens that its presence is rarely noted. But the romance is there in plenty. It lurks in the stones of every cairn, is mirrored in the face of every loch, and can be heard in the wind stirring the tops of the tall trees.

Glenmore with its rearing mountains and "Spectre of the Bloody Hand"; Rothiemurchus with its woodlands, lochs and fairy hills; the twin parishes of Abernethy and Kincardine with their countless legends; the ancient barony of Cromdale; Duthil in its "Glen of the Heroes"; Ballindalloch of the "Castle Stripe"; the Hanging Hills and Drowning Pools of the Baillie Barons; all have their tales to tell in a blend of recorded history and fanciful folklore that is a positive embarrassment of riches to the writer's pen.

Only one in every hundred of Britain's inhabitants lives north of the Grampians, and in the minds of the other ninety-nine there is generally a fixed impression that one must travel north for mountains and south for plains. In forming a mental picture of Strathspey this misconception should be eradicated right at the start, for here the exact opposite is the case, the great mountains lying to the south, with a broad swathe of fertile low country separating them from the northern sea.

Nor must it be assumed that there is only one Strathspey. Apart from a strictly geographical location, there are, in fact, several. There is the ancient land of the stone circles which the Druids called *Griannus*, Land of the Sun; the happy hunting-ground of the geologist, revelling in gneissose schist and other inanimate joys; the Mecca of the stalwart sportsman, who feels improperly dressed unless carrying a rod or gun; the nature garden of the botanist, marvelling at the beauties of a rare mountain saxifrage or the ephemeral tints in the fairy bells of an intermediate wintergreen. Lastly, there is the romantic land of the *Bodach Mor MacDuibh* and *Nighean Ban*, whose latent mysticism a visitor may feel, but only the resident can truly know.

It is with the Strathspey of romance that this narrative is chiefly concerned, but this does not mean that the story I have to tell will be completely divorced from historical fact, or that the other aspects I have mentioned will be entirely ignored. After all, botanists are not the only people who take pleasure in wild flowers, nor are ornithologists unique in being able to appreciate the song and plumage of the great variety of birds either resident in this valley or making it their summer home.

Strathspey proper lies along the forty miles of river between the two Craigellachies; the first of these being a rock at Aviemore, and the second a village and rock in Banffshire, where the river runs out into the open plain. Guide-books of the conventional sort tell us that the Spey, which rises in the Monadhliath Mountains of Inverness-shire and is 103 miles long, is the fastest-flowing river in Britain; although how this information is arrived at is never explained.

Perhaps the old log-driving days of the early nineteenth

century had something to do with justifying this claim, for it has been recorded that the time taken for floating huge rafts for sixty miles was only twelve hours. It should be remarked, however, that at one or two places—Rothiemurchus, for instance—the river's flow is so gentle as to be practically imperceptible. Here, in fact, its surface is as smooth and unruffled as a mill-pond.

One writer has called it "a black river" and a river that "grumbles and knows not song". Myopia, combined with tone-deafness, must surely have played a part in forming such an assessment, for, except when in spate (when its waters are a clay-pit red or mossy brown), like the multitude of smaller streams and burns that are its tributaries, it is remarkable for the vivid quality of its uncompromising blue. Even in the depths of winter, when the stark white of shore ice and drifting floes *can* make its waters look black and forbidding, cloudless blue skies are ever ready to come to the rescue and, by their reflected brightness, give colour and gaiety to a surface momentarily dark and cold.

The Spey may, of course, grumble on occasion, which is not surprising considering the uncomfortable, boulder-strewn route it often has to follow, but no one who has ever waded out to cast fly or lure into a pool like that at Clachnastrone could possibly make the statement that it "knows not song".

The real truth, however, is that no river worthy of the name can be expected to display uniform characteristics throughout the whole of its journey from mountain to sea. The Spey is no exception to this. Impressive in its gleaming sword-sweeps and always attractive to the eye, it is, nevertheless, no more constant in character than the course it chooses to follow.

According to the seasons, weather conditions, or the terrain it is flowing through, this river can be as capricious and unpredictable as any beautiful woman, or as turbulent and ruthless as any angry man. It can smile one moment and growl threats the next, yet it is predominantly pleasing and so strikingly individual that its like is not to be found in Scotland, or any other land.

Dependent upon the course of the river, the strath also passes through the three counties of Inverness-shire, Banffshire and Moray. There are two main routes of approach for the visitor from the south, both by road and rail. Each of these has its own special appeal. I, personally, prefer the entry from the north-east by the highly scenic little Strathspey Railway, with its fussy two-coach train jinking this way and that along a single line through a stage-set landscape of weeping-birch, rowan and pine.

The entry from the mountainous south amply illustrates the line "Caledonia, stern and wild", and while it is less welcoming it is, perhaps, the more rational route to follow if the intention is to view Strathspey as a whole. By it one can gain a quick introduction to the river while it is still little more than a rocky burn and note its gradual growth to the striking waterway it later becomes.

This southern approach entails climbing 1,400 feet to the summit of the pass through the Grampians at Drumochter, scene of the bloody fight in 1602 between the MacPhersons and Mac-Colls, when the Chief of the last-named was killed, and then travelling through the district of Badenoch, territory of the great Clan Chattan.

Despite its open, smiling freshness, Badenoch is in reality a hoarily ancient land, as its stone circles and rearing monoliths readily testify. At Raitts are to be found the "weems" of the old cave-dwellers. At Ruthven, apart from the ruins of the old barracks which witnessed so many stirring incidents during Jacobite times, can still be seen the vitrified foundations of the fortress of the *Fionn*, where the ill-natured Garaidh took his dreadful revenge.

This Garaidh, ancient tradition assures us, was a notable char-acter in more ways than one. Belonging to the *Fionn*, or Race of the Giants, he was a weakling less than ten feet tall and, as such, despised by the remainder of his tribe; particularly the women.

One day, after going out with a hunting party, the under-sized Garaidh found he could not keep up the pace of his com-panions. He went sneaking back to the stronghold at Ruthven, where he lay down by the eastern wall to refresh himself with sleep. Here some women found him in deep slumber. In a spirit of malice they pegged his long, braided hair to the ground.

When Garaidh awoke and discovered the trick that had been played upon him he flew into a berserk rage. This freed his

IN GLENMORE. On a day of reflective calm

IN ROTHIE-
MURCHUS.
In the
heart of a
peaceful
land

head, but left his hair still pegged to the ground. The women, cowed by his maddened screams, took refuge within the stronghold and barred the gate, whereupon he ringed the castle with felled trees and committed both the building and its occupants to the flames.

The warriors of the *Fionn* were hunting along the slopes of Sgorran Dhu when they saw the smoke and flames and immediately turned their earth-devouring strides towards home. When they arrived the smouldering ruins and the finding of Garaidh's hair told their own story.

Garaidh had by this time reached the Corrievairack and, considering himself at a safe distance, was setting the heavens atremble with his roar of defiance. That was his undoing. Discovering the direction he was taking, the giants set off in pursuit. They ran their quarry to earth in Wester Ross and tore him to pieces at a place which has ever since been called *Gleinn Garaidh* (Glengarry). But Garaidh had his revenge. By destroying their womenfolk he assured the extinction of the *Fionn*.

This reference to Garaidh, by the way, underlines a point that must not be overlooked. The mere mention of that old fortress immediately introduced the name of the man blamed for its destruction. This sort of twin-allusion is almost impossible to avoid when speaking of Strathspey, for there is probably nowhere else on earth, and certainly not in Britain, where land and people are so much a part of each other that it is difficult to refer to one without the other instantly assuming an equal share in the topic under discussion.

Their stories do, in fact, run strictly parallel, and this particularly applies to those inhabitants of Strathspey who answer to the name of Grant. The most prominent township in the strath is called Grantown, the Seafield-Freuchie Grants own 400,000 acres of its territory, while the Rothiemurchus Grants and MacPherson-Grants own practically all the remainder, and have done so in unbroken tenancy for hundreds of years.

The earliest known overlords in Strathspey were the Ancient Celtic Earls of Strathearn (MacLarens), and these were followed by the Comyn and Stewart Lords of Badenoch. Landowners in the upper part of the territory included members of the great Clan Chattan confederation—MacPhersons, MacKintoshes,

B

Shaws and Davidsons—while the first Grant moved in to take possession of his lands in the thirteenth century.

This prolonged close connection between land and people has been beneficial to both, especially when their welfare has been the concern of a lengthy succession of worthy and responsible Chiefs. It is impossible in a book about Strathspey not to make some reference to these, but in the interests of continuity the history of the Grants and their Chiefs has been relegated to an appendix, where they can be referred to as necessity arises.

CHAPTER II

SKELETONS, SAINTS AND FLYING BELLS

The Standard Stones of Kingussie – MacNiven and the Cave of Raitts – The Chapel of Columba – Kincraig – Loch Insh – The Bell of Insh – Other Flying Bells – Story of MacPherson of Invereshie – Loch Alvie – Concerning St. Ailbhe – The Fort at Dunachton – The Skeletons in Alvie Church – The Nighean Bean *– Other Skeletal Finds – Alvie Moor – The Tor of Alvie – The Duchess of Gordon, and Kinrara – The* Bodach Eigheach.

I HAVE already said that entry from the south, over the Grampian hump, is perhaps the better route to follow if the intention is to view Strathspey as a whole, and to this might be added that it is also the more dramatic.

No matter whether the approach from this direction is by road or rail, the effect of a tedious climb through an encompassing world of bleak and forbidding mountains is clearly felt, and the change in the rhythm of train wheels or car engine-beat is not the only evidence to convince the traveller that he has surmounted a barrier immediately the summit has been topped and left behind. This is more urgently demonstrated by the sudden burst, as from a prison's gates, into a free land of open space where fresh greens replace the sombre greys and browns, and the range of vision is expanded to take in wide, exciting stretches of open sky.

The description "free land" is used advisedly. From the moment you enter Badenoch until you leave the lower Craigellachie behind, you will not see a single "Trespass" notice in the whole of Strathspey, and can take joy in the knowledge that you are at liberty to roam where you will.

From Dalwhinnie the brooding threat of the grey Monadhliath Mountains is gradually left behind, but it is only after Newtonmore is passed that their shadow is completely erased from the memory, to be replaced by the more colourful and welcoming grace of the Monadh Ruaidh Mountains, or Cairngorms. Now you are conscious of a smiling land of sun-glinting lochs, tapestried woodlands, and rearing peaks which, though majestically *im*pressive, are just exactly the right distance away to form a background without being *op*pressive.

At Kingussie, principal township in Badenoch, you may feel an urge to linger a while. Its name comes from the Gaelic *Cean Ghiubhsaiche*, meaning "Head of the Pine Wood", and it is within handy exploring distance of places like Raitts and Ruthven. Nearby are the remains of one of the largest stone circles in the north, noted historically as the Standard Stones of the Rath of Kingussie, and it was here, in 1380, that Prince Alexander Stewart, son of King Robert II and better known as "The Wolf of Badenoch", was in the habit of holding his mods. When summoned to give evidence at one of these mods (or motes) it was customary to stand "within the circle" as an equivalent to swearing upon oath.

History has recorded for us that the Bishop of Moray refused to do this when called upon to show his titles of land tenure in the district, thereby revealing that he disputed the Wolf's jurisdiction in the matter. This refusal to acquiesce in the Lord of Badenoch's robbery of church lands, coupled with ecclesiastical disapproval of the way he treated his wife, the Countess of Buchan (because he considered her unreasonable in complaining of his preference for the Lady Mariota Athyn, mother of his five lusty, illegitimate sons), had, as its violent outcome, the turbulent Wolf's burning of the Priory at Forres and the Cathedral at Elgin.

Before the advent of the Stewarts the Comyns were the Lords of Badenoch, until their feud with Robert the Bruce led to their destruction. It is said that a Cumming dependant, named MacNiven, was responsible for the construction of the present much-visited "Cave of Raitts", although the maps name this a "Pictish" dwelling. Those who deny a Pictish origin point out that the roof of the cave is made from six-foot slabs of rock obviously taken from the great Stone Circle, and must have been made in more recent times.

It is my view that this cave is prehistoric in origin, and the fact that stones from the circle were used to roof it is only one more proof of the great antiquity of the latter erections. In other words, the circles were in existence before the cave-dwellers, whom some historians have incorrectly labelled "Picts". They were more probably the Stone Age inhabitants of Britain, who were in possession of the land before the first wave of Bronze Age Picts arrived in 1300 B.C.

There have been many theories regarding the significance of these stone circles. One investigator read into them a relation with astronomy, which has since been disproved, while a frustrated clergyman summed them up with the words: "We will say nothing more of these stones than that they have failed to hand down to us the event which they were erected to perpetuate."

No doubt this negative verdict was designed to be on the safe side, but even it is being disproved by investigations which have been going on during the past year or two. These look like establishing that the stones had a more important purpose than that of being mere memorials, and there is talk of their connection with a hitherto unknown civilization which must have been old when Egypt itself was young.

Still, tradition assures us most stoutly that, whether or not he constructed the Cave of Raitts, a MacNiven at least lived there, and the story concerning him has too much interest to be ignored.

According to the tale, this MacNiven not only dug out the cave but built a cottage over it to conceal its entrance. In the cottage he settled two ancient beldames of repulsive appearance, whose witch-like exteriors were sure to discourage visitors, and then began the business for which the whole undertaking had been planned. Having contracted with a merchant in Inverness to supply a goodly quantity of meat and hides, he now proceeded to lift these from the neighbouring MacPhersons, who were soon both baffled and infuriated at the way their cattle were disappearing, into thin air, as it seemed. Long and patiently they tracked missing beasts, until at last one of their number was struck by the circumstance that all traces of them were generally lost in the neighbourhood of the cottage occupied by the two old women.

Shortly after this the cottage's inhabitants heard a thud outside the door one night, and on going to investigate found a man lying on the doorstep. Despite their repellent appearance the women were not lacking in charity, and they soon had their unexpected visitor indoors, within range of a friendly fire. In a faint voice the intruder explained that he was dying from a chronic complaint[1] and sought only shelter from the chill night air. One of the women took out food from a cupboard and offered it to him, but he refused, whereupon she reopened the cupboard door and put the food back again. Then his benefactors retired, leaving the sick man to sleep by the fire.

When dawn came the stranger awoke, and feeling chill and hungry was reminded of the food put away on the previous evening. He went quietly to the cupboard and opened it, but instead of finding shelves containing victuals all he discovered was a dark space with a gaping hole in the floor, from which came the voices of men speaking in sepulchral tones. Hearing the women stirring in the next room, he quickly closed the cupboard door and returned to his bench by the fireplace.

Half an hour later, after thanking his hostesses, he was making his faltering way down the hill-side; but once out of view of the cottage his pretence of illness was cast aside and he ran as fast as his legs would allow to tell his MacPherson clansmen where their cattle had been going.

Needless to say, the vengeance of the plundered MacPhersons was swift and sure; but the complaint feigned by their spy is said to dog members of the clan to this day.

No doubt the Cave of Raitts has had many inhabitants in its time, but the last of whom we have definite knowledge was a vicious gang of footpads and cut-throats: dispersed after their leaders were taken and hanged at Inverness in 1773.

In the fifteenth century the Lordship of Badenoch was granted by King James II to the Gordon Earl of Huntly, and shortly after this the Old Priory of Kingussie was built. In 1718 the British Government saw fit to erect a strong, fortified barracks on the site of an earlier castle, but the rising of "the '45" saw the end of this also, and now nothing but a roofless, fire-scarred shell remains.

In an old kirkyard can be found a memorial stone marking the site of the ancient chapel personally founded by St. Columba. It is set in the wall, under an arch of clustering ivy, with a holy-water stoup acting as its base.

[1] The Gaelic name for this was *Galar-fuil*.

Following the main North Road the next little township is Kincraig, one of the most cheating, and yet most delightful, villages anywhere along the banks of the Spey. From the main highway it appears trim but undistinguished, but, viewed from the road on the far side of the river, it is a very different story. From here you will note with a feeling of unbelief its two pine-crested peninsulas running out into Loch Insh with, on one of them, the nestling white church, built on the site of the ancient Chapel of the Swans.

The name Insh comes from the Gaelic *Innis* (an island), and at one time these peninsulas *were* islands; as, indeed, one of them still is when the Spey, which flows in at one end of Loch Insh and out at the other, is in spate. Above them, up a winding track, is a tree-clad mound where one can sit and, without any great strain on the imagination, look down the ages to the days when warring Pict and Northman fought on land once sacred to the Druid of a still earlier era.

I last sat there on an October afternoon of typical autumn calm, watching a whole flock of mute swans, proud frigates with white sails full spread, acting as escort to a slower-moving convoy of mallard, widgeon and goosander. My surroundings were the very epitome of peace, and it seemed strange that on such a breathless day so many feathered ships could tack and cruise without the slightest puff of wind to help them on their way.

Within the little church is a particularly rare Celtic treasure, a flying bell, similar to the Bell of St. Fillan which, I understand, now rests on a little island in Loch Shiel. There used to be another bell of this type at Ardchattan, known as St. Modan's Bell. This had the same qualities as the Bell of Insh, in that it could find its own way home after being lent to distant parishes for healing purposes, and was also able to sing in flight.

The Bell of Insh once flew back all the way from Perth, singing its homing song "*Tom-an-Eunan, Tom-an-Eunan*", the old name of the mound on which the bell's sanctuary still stands; but the Bell of St. Modan was less fortunate when returning from Scone. Being jostled by a flock of starlings, it changed the words of its homing song to "*An rud nach bhuin duit, na bhuin da*" ("Touch not those who touch not you"), and thus went off its course to meet a fate that has never since been discovered.

Nowadays the Bell of Insh is kept in a stone cup within the

church, and to assure that its flying days are over it is securely chained—a necessary precaution in this "civilized" age when it is not only supernatural agencies that make objects of veneration or historical interest fly. It can, however, still be seen and handled, and this, considering its healing powers, is something; but woe betide those who insist on hearing it sing, for every clanging note from its iron tongue brings a year of bad luck to the ringer.

On the eastern shore of the loch, and across the river, lies the secondary road running all the way from Grantown to Newton-more and beyond, its surface well metalled and serving an area rich both in scenic beauty and romance. This road must be followed if a closer view is desired of Invereshie and Dalnavert, ancient homes of MacPhersons and Shaws respectively. Invereshie House can, in fact, be seen nestling among its trees from the little mound just mentioned, and it was near here that the celebrated MacPherson the Reiver was born, a Laird of Invereshie being his natural father.

These MacPherson lairds apparently had a ready eye for feminine charm, and an interesting story is told concerning one of them who succumbed to the beauty of the alluring Miss Shaw of Dalnavert.

The wedding of this couple was marked by lavish celebration, and some say that this set the tone for the scale on which the young bride decided to live for ever after. Whether or not this be true, she certainly had the most expensive tastes, and her generosity was exercised to such a profligate degree that a day came when, in spite of her husband's remonstrances, she had succeeded in bringing the once wealthy estate to the verge of ruin. Treasured woodlands were felled and the timber sold, but the situation did not improve.

The Laird, in desperation, decided that something drastic had to be done to alter his wife's ways, but could not, for the life of him, think of a suitable course to follow. Then one night, after a more than usually angry scene, his lady resolved the matter for him by stamping out of the house with the avowed intention of returning to her father without letting another hour pass over her head.

Fuming with indignation she got as far as the River Feshie to find the ford obliterated in a rush of spating waters. The only prudent thing to do was to return to the house and postpone her departure till the morrow, but prudence was the one quality she lacked most in her infuriated mood of the moment, and sooner than return to her husband's possible jeers she plunged blindly ahead.

Of course she had gone only a pace or two from the bank when the weight of waters swept her from her feet and sent her hurtling towards the all-consuming Spey. But, for once in her life, the fact that she had always insisted upon being a fashionable lady stood her in good stead, for, wearing the stylish number of flounced petticoats, these buoyed her up for just long enough to let her grasp the trailing branch of a riverside tree.

She was still hanging on to this when her husband, out for a stroll in an endeavour to cool his ire, came upon her. As soon as she saw him she called out urgently for aid, but he was evidently in no hurry to comply. He stood pondering for a moment, then whipping his dirk from its scabbard he began hacking at her support, crying:

"You have taken the best of my trees, you may as well have this branch along with the rest."

It was only when he saw his wife actually being swept away that the enormity of his act fully dawned upon him, and it is comforting to record that he wasted no further time in jumping into the flood to rescue her.

It is said that this demonstration of ruthlessness in her once pliable husband had a very chastening effect upon the lady, and that thereafter she led a most affectionate and economic existence; so much so that when her son, Æneas, came of age he was able to look upon a patrimony reasonable to behold.

Crossing back to the western side of the river, and still following the main highway, a short two and a half miles downstream will bring the traveller to the little church and loch of Alvie.

Away back in the long ago there were three chapels in the parish of Alvie, the first dedicated to St. Eatha, at Kinrara, the second to St. Drostan, at Dunachton, and the third to St. Maluac, at Balavil. The main church, however, poised on a peninsula running out into Loch Alvie, was dedicated to St. Ailbhe, from whom the parish takes its name.

St. Ailbhe, like most of his saintly brethren of the old Culdean Church, had a truly eventful career, in the Celtic *genre*. His father was Olchu, and his mother a maidservant who loved not wisely but too well. On becoming aware of her pregnancy, and fearing the wrath of her righteous master, Cronan, she fled. But the arm of Cronan stretched far, and her son was no sooner born than an order arrived from her master that the child had to be exposed upon the hill-side. The mother had no choice but to obey, her only concession to maternal instinct being to place him under the shelter of a rock; hence his name, for the Gaelic *Ail* means " a rock ".

A few days later Lochlan, son of Laidhir, while out hunting, found the babe being suckled by a wolf and took him home to his wife who, strangely enough, had a name similar to Ailbhe's father in that it had the same meaning " evil ". This, however, was just one more occasion when evil was used to bring forth good. The sea-going Lochlan disposed of the boy to a tribe of Britons, who had him baptized, and the next we hear of him he is setting out on the long pilgrimage to Rome.

On his return to Britain St. Ailbhe founded a monastery, whose location can no longer be identified. A few years later he was at the court of the Dalriadan King, Fintan Finn, whom he obliged by retrieving his wife and children, taken captive by the men of Connacht. His manner of carrying out this was both simple and forthright. All he did was curse the Connacht men so roundly and continuously that they sickened of the sound of his voice and were at last glad to let their prisoners go for the sake of a little peace and quiet.

When returning to Ireland from the court of Fintan Finn, St. Ailbhe passed through Strathspey, where he founded the holy cell by the Loch of Alvie. In Ireland he settled his disciple, St. Colman (noted at a later date in wordy conflict with St. Columba over the question of Dalriadan independence),[1] and then went on to pay a visit to St. Bridget of Kildare.

It is noteworthy that St. Colman had as adviser St. Eatha, known as the " St. Bridget of Munster ", and it was to her that the little chapel at Kinrara was dedicated. No trace of this now remains, nor of the earlier edifice raised by St. Ailbhe, but the ruins of St. Drostan's chapel at Dunachton can still be seen.

Dunachton, by the way, means Nachtan's Fort, and is so named after that Nachtan (or Nectan), King of the Picts, who won a

[1] See *In the Steps of the Clansmen*, p. 24.

great victory over the Norsemen at the Battle of Nectan's Mere. The Clan MacNaughton trace their descent from this king.

The present Church of Alvie has known much rebuilding and alteration. In Reformation days, after being taken over from the Church of Rome, its altar was removed, and, at a much later date, so also was the box-like gallery on the side wall where the Duke and Duchess of Gordon used to sit above their tenantry. In 1880 some alterations were being carried out which necessitated removing dry-rotted board from the floor, and great was the surprise of the workmen when they found 150 skeletons, lying head to head, immediately under the floor-boards. The bones were collected and transferred to the outer kirkyard, where a cross now marks the spot of the re-interment. On this cross are the words:

> " Who they were, when they lived, how they died,
>   Tradition notes not."

> " *Their bones are dust, their good swords rust,*
>   *Their souls are with the saints we trust.*"

To the first part of this memorial might have been added " and we care not ", because no real effort appears to have been made to establish the identity of the recumbent host.

An old tradition has it that the *Nighean Bean* was once seen on the shores of Loch Alvie washing the blood from many shirts and spreading them out to dry on boulders by the loch shore. As she worked she complained loudly over the size of her task, and as this supernatural creature had the exclusive duty of washing the shirts of those about to be slain, the very mention of her presence suggests a battle in the immediate neighbourhood.

My personal wish is that those skeletons committed to a common grave over seventy years ago should be dug up and cephalic measurements taken. My own theory is that these remains are very old indeed, and I shall explain my reason for so thinking.

These are not the only human skeletons that have been found in this particular neighbourhood. Earthen tumuli and stone cairns abound, and the chances are that these were even more numerous at one time than they are to-day. When one of these, directly opposite the church, was opened about a hundred years ago it contained the skeleton of a large man across whose breast was laid a pair of hart horns of uncommon size. My view is that when the church was being built a number of tumuli were already occupying the desired site, and that when the masons were removing these the skeletons were uncovered. One can almost hear them tell the incoming priest of their find, and that merciful man's decision to bless the unknown dead with holy water and leave them where they lay, building his church immediately over them.

If this really was the case, it seems sad that a minister of another creed should one day find them and expel them from the hallowed haven in which they had rested so long.

On Alvie Moor there are traces of a Roman Camp, and Roman urns under arches of partly-baked clay have been found there. Add to this the ruins of the fort built by King Nachtan, and recall the considerable number of Norse names scattered all over the strath, and the possibility of at least one large and gory battle being fought around Alvie is easily imagined.

Now, however, all is peace along the shores of the mile-long loch, and the only excitement I have ever experienced there lay in watching the multitudinous water-lilies open their sweet smiling faces to greet the coming of day and an early rising summer sun.

Once, when enjoying a scrambling walk over the hills behind Delfour, I paused on the rocky slopes of *An-Squabach* to look down at Loch Alvie, divided from the hill-foot by only a cotton-blossomed marsh. The church and its sheltering trees were mirrored in the still, gleaming water with no more distortion than could be found in a looking-glass, and even a long-distance motor-coach gliding along the Inverness road could not quite destroy the timeless beauty of the scene.

My gaze roved on, taking in the stone circle at Delfour, past the pine wood at Dalraddy and across the river to the Tor of Alvie. Here was encountered the first cause for annoyance, for not only does this rearing, tree-clad mount—beautiful enough in itself—obstruct the view to Glenmore, but it also bears on its crest the memorial to the last Duke of Gordon. This is a fitting product of the age which could, quite needlessly, disturb and remove the bones of the venerable dead. A round, towering pillar, shooting straight up from the trees, it might have looked quite in keeping if placed in Glasgow's Necropolis or the square of some north-country English spa, but here it is no more than an excrescence that makes one wonder why Jove should squander his bolts on harmless hayricks while this defiance to his might still stands. Lacking any measure of beauty, it is not even down-right ugly—it is just *stupid*—and no doubt that is what makes it so hard to bear.

Closing my eyes and cutting the annoyance from view, I allowed my mind to dwell a moment on the other memorials I knew those Kinrara trees to hold; the cairn commemorating the valour of the Black Watch and Gordon Highlanders at the Battle of Waterloo, and, down by the river, the strange, box-like mausoleum of the gay and charming Lady Jane, Duchess of Gordon.

The Lady Jane loved Kinrara, along whose roads she used to drive in a phaeton drawn by gaily-caparisoned goats, and it is no doubt fitting that she should choose to leave her earthly remains here. But surely she could have known nothing of this ridiculous stone shell in which her coffin was to be housed.

Darkness was falling when I got down from the hills, reached the main road, and set off towards Aviemore where a train would take me on the major part of my way home. I stepped out at a good pace, not with any concern that I might miss my train, but because I knew that Alvie has more than charm to offer the stranger with the coming of night. There is, for instance, the *Bodach Eigheach*, who, dog at heel, can still be heard wailing his death-call over moon-rippled waters, warning those unfortunate enough to hear him that one more soul is about to go winging on its way.

CHAPTER III

ROADS AND REIVERS

P R O B A B L Y no district in the Scottish Highlands is better
served with highways than Strathspey, and even if they sometimes lack the width and straightness demanded in this age of
the *autobahnen* they are at least well-surfaced and never dull
to travel upon; it being impossible to guess what lies over the
next hill or around the next bend. Yet the main roads should
be used with discretion, as a necessary means of getting quickly
from one place to another, the secondary, less-frequented
byways through forest and moorland proving so much more
satisfying.

South of Kingussie stretches an old Drover's Road, a General
Wade's Road, and the permanent way of British Railways; all
running parallel with the main highway, but at different levels.
This creates an optical illusion which makes the car-driver
imagine he is coasting, when the normal opposite is the case.
But, despite the interest this occasions, the less-populous
thoroughfares, with their singing, tree-lined burns and woodlands offering companionable escort, are still to be preferred.

This particularly applies to the routes from Grantown to
Aberlour, on the way to Elgin. Here the main road may be
termed scenically perfect, but it is much more difficult to find
suitable adjectives of praise when describing the narrower, little-
used, but well-surfaced highway on the opposite side of the river.
The motorist can, however, appreciate both by travelling as far

as Craigellachie on one road and returning to Grantown by the other; a round trip of about fifty miles.

The earliest known road-builder in Strathspey was King Alexander II. Traces of a road he made in 1236 can still be seen south of Staor-na-mannoch (the Monk's Bridge), near Tulloch, where people with the Gaelic still continue to call it *Rathad-an-Righ* (the King's Road).

There is some confusion over King Alexander's successors in this work. The ordnance maps show sections of what are termed Roman Roads, but there is no reliable authority for giving them such an origin. The more feasible explanation is that these old roads were built by the Kirk, who used the fines extracted from wrongdoers for this purpose. In support of this it can be stated that the so-called "Roman" road at Congash at one time probably passed a former dwelling of mine, which, interestingly enough, is recorded in the County Clerk's books under the very old address: "Kirk Road, Strathspey, Cromdale." This, it should be noted, bears no relation whatever to the address recognized by the postal authorities, and no one living in this district has any recollection of a "Kirk Road" ever having existed here.

The most celebrated road-builder in this area was undoubtedly General Wade who, by 1770, was estimated to have laid over 800 miles of Highland roads and built upwards of 1,000 bridges. Remains of the Wade roads in Strathspey are legion, and there is one particularly charming thoroughfare in Grantown still known as "General Wade's Road". This runs straight up from the banks of the Spey at Clach-na-Strone, and continues through the great trees of the Anagach Wood to end in Forest Road no more than 300 yards from the centre of the town.

Another variety of road here, far from unique in the Highlands, is the old type of Drover Road (used by cattle-dealers until last century), lineal descendants of still older roads that were used for a less lawful, but much more stirring purpose—that of cattle-lifting. The most famous of these, *Rathad-nam-Mearlach*, the Thieves' Road, passes right across the most mountainous regions of Strathspey from west to east. By it raiders from faraway Lochaber crossed the Monadhliath range, travelled through Rothiemurchus, skirted the south shore of Loch Morlich, and passed out of Glenmore at Loch-an-Uaine (the

Green Loch). Beyond this it traversed Strath Avon and the Garioch right down to where the eastern shores of Scotland are met by the North Sea.

A formidable route to follow, especially when having to move quickly with stolen cattle; yet a magnificent one, in all ways worthy of the hardy and daring men who chose to follow the calling of *kernachan*.

To their Lowland victims these caterans appeared as nothing more attractive than "lawless limmers", and just how much they were feared is shown by a litany recited at Dunkeld Cathedral. This placed the reivers first of all evils in a supplication which, translated from the Latin, reads: "From caterans and robbers, from wolves and all wild beasts, Lord deliver us."

Yet to the Highlanders, who looked upon the men of the low country as a usurping, alien race whom they scornfully called "*Sassenach*", there was nothing dishonest in lifting cattle fattened on land they believed to be rightfully their own.

Mention of the word "*Sassenach*" makes me wonder who was first to deduce that it means "Saxon". Writers have been blandly assuming this translation for a long time now, yet the term was applied to all Lowlanders, Scots as well as English, and simply means "a fat, gluttonous fellow". This is the definition given in all old Gaelic dictionaries, and surely these offer more authoritative guidance than the English dictionaries of to-day.

We know, of course, how proud the Southerner has always been of "the roast beef of old England", and can also understand how scornful the spartan Highlander would be of a people so boastfully preoccupied with the subject of food, but to avoid any possibility of being considered impolite I, personally, am always most careful never to allude to my fellow-Briton south of the border as a *Sassenach*.

Strathspey is rich in tales of *spreachs*, or cattle forays, and the first traditional mention of such an undertaking concerns an incursion of Camerons, from Lochaber, early in the sixteenth century. On this occasion the men of Tulloch were down in Forres collecting a millstone, and as this had to be rolled along with a pole through its middle for almost forty miles the man-power needed for the task was considerable. This meant that

COYLUM BRIDGE. Haunt of the Cleocain Dearg

IN THE PASS OF
REVOAN

Where the Thieves'
Road skirts the
Green Loch

when the raiders struck there was only the bowman (as the cattle-herd was called) to offer opposition; but it so happened that this guard, known as *Fear-na-casan-caol* (now remembered as "The Thin Man"), was noted for his swiftness as a runner, and he made good use of this accomplishment when summoning aid.

Covering the ground at an amazing rate he caught the men of Rothiemurchus as they were leaving church after the Sunday service and, enlisting their help, started leading them towards a point of interception. Alas, his extraordinary turn of speed, coupled with a certain hot-headedness, proved the worthy bow-man's undoing. Finding he had outstripped the support he had recruited, and too rash to await their arrival, he struck at the Camerons single-handed—with the inevitable result. When the avenging Grants arrived on the scene they found their cattle intact, but of raiders and bowman there was no sign.

As the months went by there was much speculation as to what could have happened to the missing herdsman. Then one day a woman who had been visiting relatives in Lochaber arrived in Tulloch. She was able to dispel the mystery, having overheard the Cameron raiders tell how they had slain the impetuous bow-man and hurriedly buried him at a certain spot near Loch Eanaich. Search was quickly made here and the remains of the "Swift One" duly discovered.

A footnote to this old tradition is that in the early part of the present century an antique *sgian*, or knife, was found near the reputed site of the bowman's grave, suggesting that the tale was not entirely lacking in foundation.

Shortly after this the Camerons again made a bid for the cattle of Tulloch, choosing a time when all the local menfolk were celebrating the wedding of the tacksman at Delnapoit. The only intimation the Strathspey men had of this raid was when they went out in the morning after a long night's feasting and found the cattle-folds empty, but they wasted not a moment in preparing pursuit, and a force was soon mustered under the leadership of Alan Grant of Auchernach.

Once more the Camerons were out of luck, for the Grants caught them resting by the Slochd of Bachdarn and, having the advantage of the hill, immediately attacked. The reivers were forced to retreat, leaving all their spoils behind, but not before

C

their leader, Ian Dubh, had his nose split by an arrow from Grant of Auchernach, an expert in the use of the short Highland bow. Ever after this Ian Dubh was known as *Iain Dubh biorach*, " Dark Ian of the sharp nose "; and he was not at all the sort of man to accept such disfigurement without making some effort to obtain revenge.

At last the chance Ian Dubh had been waiting for duly arrived. Alan of Auchernach had a public quarrel with the priest of Finlarig over a matter of precedence while both were waiting to have their meal ground at Drummaille Mill. In his anger Auchernach made certain ambiguous threats, and this his enemy determined to profit by. Stealing up to the priest's house in the dead of the night, Ian Dubh stabbed the old man to the heart, and then left events to take their normal course.

As might be expected, there was a great outcry over this brutal murder, and after his threats to the priest Grant of Auchernach was immediately suspected. He was arrested by order of the Bishop of Moray, taken to Elgin, and thrown into prison. Committed to the torture chamber he bore his ordeal bravely, and was still protesting his innocence when relegated to a dungeon pending further interrogation.

Shortly after this Ian Dubh, who had long been an outlaw, was apprehended for another killing and sentenced to be hanged. Before his death he made a confession proving Auchernach's innocence, and tradition tells us that the Bishop compensated the wrongfully accused Alan by settling him in the lands of Muck-rach; thus forming a new branch of the clan, to-day represented by the Grants of Rothiemurchus.

That is the old tale, but history, unfortunately, does not bear it out. We know that the first Grant of Muckrach was named Patrick, not Alan, and that the Grants of Muckrach were known as Clan Patrick, while those of Auchernach were called Clan Alan. The story of how the Muckrach Grants moved to Rothie-murchus will be told later on.

Another version of the above traditional story was put forward by Sir Thomas Dick Lauder in a tale entitled *The Rival Lairds*, and here the licence of the romantic novelist was allowed full rein. In this rendering Alan became Lewis Grant of Auchernach, a fair-haired Galahad betrothed to the niece of the vener-able priest of Duthil, while his rival for the maiden's hand,

Ian Dubh, instead of being a Cameron, becomes the dark-avised Black John Grant, Laird of Knockando. The priest is duly murdered and Auchernach wrongfully accused, but it is the faith and detective instincts of the beautiful Helen, the priest's niece, and not any confession on the real murderer's part, that save the innocent Auchernach from paying the penalty for another man's crime.

The most notable cattle-raid concerning the men of Strathspey, although it did not actually take place here, was the celebrated Raid of Moyness. This also has the added attraction of being strictly verified by documentary record, and once more the Camerons were the culprits; although instead of coming into Strathspey on this occasion they chose for their depredation a Grant holding in the Laigh of Moray.

According to a contemporary written account, news of the raid was quickly received in Strathspey and a pursuing force mustered under the command of Grant of Lurg. Again the Camerons were overtaken, and Lurg sent forward "Mickle" Lawson, ancestor of the Lawsons of Balliemore, with the demand that the reivers retire, leaving the cattle behind, to prevent bloodshed. The wild Cameron clansmen showed nothing but scorn for such a humanitarian plea, and as Lawson was returning with their answer one of the fierce Lochaber men loosed an arrow and killed him.

Grant of Lurg thereupon ordered the Strathspey men to attack. Greatly aided by the prowess of a famous bowman, a Grant who worked for Mr. MacKintosh of Kylachie, they routed the raiders, killing eight and wounding twelve, as well as recovering the stolen cattle in full.

A letter to the Laird of Grant from Lochiel, retained in the Grant muniment chest, casts further light on this encounter. As some readers find the old spelling and idiom tiresome, I am putting the letter forward in this modern rendering:

" Allan Cameron of Lochiel to Sir James Grant of Freuchie.
Glenlocharbeg, 18th October, 1645.

RIGHT HONOURABLE AND LOVING COUSIN,
May my hearty commendations be remembered to your worship. I have received your letter concerning the unfortun-

ate affair that has involved our houses, the like of which has
never before been encountered in any man's day. But, praise
be to God, I and my friends are innocent of any intention to
harm your worship, because when we went to Morayland,
where all men take their prey, we had no idea that Moyness
was a Grant possession. Had we really known this, we should
not have disturbed it any more than we would think of inter-
fering with your worship's other possessions in Strathspey. As it
is, I have suffered such loss among my friends—eight of whom
are already dead, with a further twelve or thirteen under cure
and no man knowing whether they will live or die—that I am
sure your worship will take this into consideration and realize
that it is I, not you, who has suffered the greatest loss in this
affair.

Refraining from troubling you further at this time, and
knowing that your worship will not be offended by my thus
proclaiming the innocence of my friends,

So I rest yours,

ALLAN CAMERONE OF LOCHYLL."

The reference to Morayland in this letter, which I have noted
in italics, is worthy of attention, showing as it does the viewpoint of the old Highland Chief. Morayland was in the Lowlands, *ergo*, it is designated fair game and a place "where all
men take their prey".

The different ways in which Lochiel writes his name in this
letter also demands note. It marks the lack of uniformity in
spelling at this time, and is a chastening reminder to those who
claim there is only one *correct* way to spell a given name.

Another interesting outcome of this raid was the clan inquest
that followed. This brought to book the young Grant laird of
the old Ballindalloch family for withdrawing from the fight, and
made him face a charge of cowardice before the Clan Elders.
His punishment was that he had to attend church service at
Inverallan every Sunday for a whole year, listen to the Kylachie
bowman say after the sermon: "I am the man who acquitted
himself valiantly at Moyness," and then himself stand up and
make the reply: "I am the man who acted the coward's part on
that occasion."

This power of the Clan Elders to discipline erring chieftains is too often lost sight of by those who regard clan chiefship as an absolute, rather than a benevolent, despotism. It was, admittedly, only used on rare occasions; nevertheless, it was a safeguard in protecting the interests and welfare of the humbler clansmen.

A noteworthy example of this protection by the Clan Elders was their manner of dealing with a certain young Laird of Lurg. This youth, known as " The Lieutenant ", was utterly irresponsible and licentious in his manner of life, and succeeded in dissipating a very large patrimony. Accompanied by a band of kindred spirits he would descend upon this tenant or that and billet his whole band of libertines until they had eaten and drunk the household out of all provision, then move on to the steading of the next unwilling host. At last his conduct could be tolerated no longer, and the much-abused tenantry appealed to the Clan Elders to rid them of their troublesome Laird.

With some clans this might have meant the use of a dirk on a dark night, but the Grants, despite their prowess in battle, always liked, when possible, to keep on the right side of the law. The method the Clan Elders took of dealing with the present situation underlines this. They simply went quietly round the countryside buying up the profligate chieftain's debts until these reached a sum they knew he could not possibly meet, then they had him arrested and removed to a debtor's prison. Later, he was forced to take refuge in the Sanctuary at Holyrood, where he died on December 21st, 1821.

When remarking that the inhabitants of Strathspey were as a rule inclined to be law-abiding, we have, of course, also to remember the exceptions, without which no rule can be proved. Outstanding among these was James Grant, " The Reiver of Carron ", whose Gaelic name was *Seumais-an-tuim* (James of the Hill), as desperate a cateran as any district in the Highlands could lay claim to.

The general feeling of the authorities in Edinburgh was that the Laird of Grant was not pursuing this kinsman outlaw with all the desired relentlessness, and as the reiver was operating at a time when Strathspey was harvesting quite a crop of law-breakers (early seventeenth century), he was not lacking in accomplices. The first real check to his career came when he was making one of many raids into Badenoch and was surprised by Clan Chattan,

who killed four of his men and took him prisoner, bleeding from
many wounds. He was conveyed to Edinburgh, where he was
incarcerated in the castle, but in 1632, aided by his wife, who
smuggled him lengths of rope concealed in casks of butter, he
made a spectacular escape and returned to Strathspey, more or
less carrying on his activities as before.

At last, hunted on every side, and with most of his allies taken,
he and his small band sought shelter one night in a cottage in
Strathbogie, not knowing their refuge was the dwelling of the
common hangman. One can well imagine the feelings of the
latter when he saw such a crop of " tree-fruits " come to his hand
for the plucking, or picture the eagerness with which he sent one
of his womenfolk to the baillie with the request that the house
be surrounded. But the watch kept by the Carron men was too
alert to permit of surprise. One of them noted the woman's
absence and, making a shrewd guess at the reason for it, saw
that he and his companions had slipped quietly away before the
baillie's men arrived.

Shortly after this it was given out that *Seumais-an-tuim* had
been killed in a fight, but there is probably more truth in the
contrary statement that he died in his bed in 1639.

The fate of another Strathspey cateran, Peter Roy MacGregor,
was more certain, and this description of him by Lord Pitmeddie
can serve as his epitaph:

" He was of low stature, but strong made, had a fierce countenance, a brisk, hawk-like eye. He bore the torture of the boots
with great constancy, and was undaunted at his execution,
although mangled by the executioner in cutting off his hand."

This Peter Roy was notorious for activities other than reiving,
and is credited with having exercised an amazing power over
women. Local superstition attributed this to a " love-spot " on
his cheek, similar to that borne by the mythological Diarmid on
his brow, but whatever the explanation, the fascination he had
for the fair sex was such that they were not even jealous of one
another when it came to seeking his favours. The first time he
was apprehended and taken to Edinburgh the women of Tullochgorm managed to raise the sum of one hundred crowns for his
ransom; but when arrested for the second time their menfolk
took good care that they were not informed until their loved
one had already met his end.

Another notable MacGregor reiver at this period also came from Tullochgorm. He was Iain Dhu Gear (Swift Dark Ian),[1] but as I have already told his tragic story elsewhere I will not repeat it here; contenting myself with the reminder that Mac-Jockie Grant and his two sons, Patrick and John, were hanged for aiding and abetting him.[2]

Alistair Grant of Wester Tulloch, a close ally of the Reiver of Carron, was either a son or brother of MacJockie. Accompanied by John Grant of Carron, nephew of *Seumais-an-tuim*, he was responsible for the murder of Lachlan MacKintosh and Thomas Grant of Dalvey in 1628. Having been put to the horn as an outlaw he escaped to the Glynns of Antrim (surely, as discussed in Appendix I, another indication of a connection between the Grants and this part of the world), and a letter from Lord Antrim still exists commending him to the Laird of Grant.

This Grant laird, as it happened, had also received a communication of another kind regarding Alistair. This was a commission from the Crown ordering the Grant Chief to pursue his lawless clansman and "use all kinds of force and warrlyke ingyne" to effect his capture. This the Laird, Sir John, succeeded in doing, and Alistair was lodged in the Tolbooth, Edinburgh, in 1631.

After several postponements, Alistair's case was brought before the Judges on August 4th, 1632. John Grant of Ballindalloch and a Grant of Dalvey were his chief accusers. He was charged with the slaughter of Thomas Grant and Lachlan MacKintosh on the lands of Rothiemoon in August, 1628; with having raided Inverernan, taking away kine, oxen, ewes and other plenishings in November, 1628; and with slaying John Dallas during an attack on Ballindalloch on April 23rd, 1630. He was found guilty on all counts and sentenced to death, but the Laird of Grant and other influential friends procured an Act of Council to postpone his execution, and this, in fact, was never carried out.

The most mysterious of all Strathspey's outlaws was, undoubtedly, *An Gamhainn Cirinn*, "The Halkit Stirk"; probably so named because of some facial peculiarity. The true identity of this freebooter has never been fully established, but there is good reason to believe he was a Glencoe or Glengarry Mac-

---

[1] See pp. 164-166 of *In the Steps of the Clansmen*.
[2] The name 'MacJockie' is nowadays pronounced 'MacCook' in Strathspey.

Donald from the west. Once, when apprehended, the Laird of Grant, his captor, sent a letter to the Committee of Estates pointing out the great danger of reprisals from the McDonalds if ill befell the prisoner. In reply the Estates assured him that they would be very willing to "resent and repair any wrong that shall be done to you or your followers upon this accompt", while also instructing that the prisoner be delivered to the magistrates at Aberdeen, who would forward him under strong guard to the Tolbooth at Edinburgh.

The Halkit Stirk was so delivered, but his friends in Strathspey did not desert him. They even got the Laird of Grant to transmit a petition to the Lord Advocate "to speak for the Halkit Stirk to see if he will be releivit upon good securitie".

At a time when the Highlands were already greatly disturbed, the Estates, not wishing to give further cause for clan feuds, released their prisoner upon the security offered, and he was soon back in Strathspey continuing his old activities. During a spulzie at the Green Loch he was badly wounded and left in the care of the Stewarts, foresters at Glenmore.

The Stirk, an interesting and far from troublesome guest, was soon on terms of the greatest friendliness with all members of the household giving him succour. One day, while regarding her youngest son, he remarked to Mrs. Stewart:

"That's a fine, manly lad you've got there. I would say he's ready for school."

On Mrs. Stewart assuring her guest that the boy had already been to school at Ruthven and done very well there, the Stirk replied:

"*Cha'n e Sgoile a phaiper gheall bha mi ciallachadh, ach sgoile-na-geallich*" ("It is not the school of the white paper I am thinking of, but the school of the moon").

The Halkit Stirk, an outlaw very much in the Robin Hood tradition, died in old age. On his deathbed he is reputed to have said:

"I have never taken from the poor, I have never been other than kind to the widow and the fatherless, and I have always travelled far from the property of my friends in search of spoil."

Another freebooter well known in Strathspey was the celebrated James MacPherson, sometimes dubbed "The Rob Roy of

LOOKING ACROSS DORBACK. A roadside view of the Cairngorms

STRAND AT LOCH MORLICH. Where Robin Og met the "Bloody Hand"

HOME OF THE
KELPIE

Lovely Loch
Pityoulish in
early spring

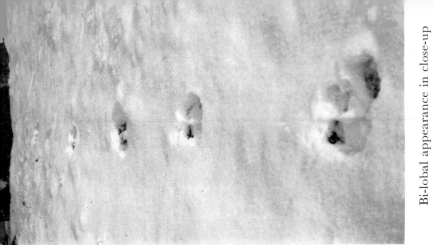

Bi-lobal appearance in close-up

THE MYSTERIOUS TRACKS. Note unusual size

the North ". Burns wrote a song about him, and Sir Walter Scott made notes with a view to weaving a romance round his colourful life, only failing health preventing him from carrying out his intention.

This MacPherson was the natural son of a Laird of Invershie and a beautiful, red-haired tinker lass. His boyhood was spent almost equally between his father's turbulent clansmen and the free, wandering journeys of his mother's vagrant race. Having such a background, it is not surprising that he loved the open-air life and became leader of a band of raiders whose activities were a plague to dwellers in the Lowlands.

MacPherson was noted for his beauty, strength and stature. Like Rob Roy he was famed as a swordsman, but, unlike him, he favoured the old, two-handed claymore rather than the more fashionable broadsword. His own particular weapon was of such a size that few men could carry it for any distance, let alone wield it in battle. And, next to his swordsmanship and daring, he was lauded for his abilities as violinist and composer. He could translate into music his every mood, and many of his compositions are still played at the present day.

The very fact that Scott contemplated writing a novel about him proves the extent of his exploits. Among these, his escape from the death cell in Aberdeen was one of the most thrilling. He had been captured by treachery, and the serving maid of an Aberdeen magistrate sent word of his plight to his friends. This brought to Aberdeen the outlaw's cousin, Donald MacPherson, accompanied by a tinker member of the band, named Peter Brown.

When Donald and Peter reached the town they found a scaffold already erected flush with the prison wall, and the execution timed to take place at noon on the following day. The hour for the hanging was carefully chosen, because MacPherson was known to have many sympathizers among the poorer folk in Aberdeen, and the intention was to have his death witnessed by as many of these as possible. Finding the city too well guarded for a rescue by storm, the condemned man's two friends pinned their faith on an audacious plan whose only virtue lay in its element of surprise.

About an hour before the scheduled execution Donald and Peter, moving in a throng of sightseers, reached the scaffold.

Without a moment's hesitation they ran up the steps on to its platform and knocked at a small door in the prison wall. When this was opened by a warder, Donald, a man of herculean strength, felled him with his sword-hilt. Peter then snatched the gaoler's keys and darted inside to the adjoining condemned cell where he knew his master would be housed.

All this was witnessed by the crowd, but there is no doubt where their sympathies lay, and in all that throng there was only one man, a butcher, who was sufficiently tempted by the thought of possible reward to try foiling the rescue. This fellow mounted a staircase overlooking the scaffold until he reached a point above Donald's head, then he launched his whole weight down upon him.

There followed a fight of the utmost ferocity, for the butcher, like Donald, was a powerfully-built man. In the midst of the battle Peter came out of the prison carrying his leader, who was still bound by manacles and fetters. It was just then that the butcher's bull-dog, attracted by its master's cries, came charging up from a nearby yard to take part in the fight.

Donald, with wits as quick as his fists, whipped off his plaid and threw it round his opponent. The scent of this confused the dog and caused it to attack its master. While the butcher was striving to free himself from strong jaws clamped to his thigh the rescuers seized their chance to get down into the crowd.

The populace showed their friendship by staging brawls among themselves to distract the attention of the soldiery hurrying to the scene. Under cover of this diversion MacPherson was carried to an inn where horses were waiting. Here he was freed from his fetters, and the fugitives were soon dashing past a surprised gate-guard to the safety of the hills.

Alas, unlike Rob Roy or the Halkit Stirk, MacPherson was neither fated to know old age nor granted the dubious pleasure of dying in his bed. Betrayed by a secret enemy, he was captured and hanged at Banff, the last person in Scotland to be executed under the mandate of heritable jurisprudence.

He was granted one boon: leave to play his violin for the last time. Starting with his famous "MacPherson's Rant", he ended with "MacPherson's Farewell", then he took his violin in both hands and shattered it across his knee. A member of the crowd picked up the neck of the broken instrument and conveyed it to Donald MacPherson. He passed it on to his Chief, Cluny MacPherson, in whose ancestral home it is still preserved.

Robert Burns, in his song "MacPherson's Farewell", depicts the freebooter's last moments on earth and conveys something of the gay defiance of the scene:

> " Sae rantingly, sae wantonly,
>   Sae dauntingly gaed he;
>   He played a spring and danced it round,
>   Beneath the gallows tree."

CHAPTER IV

THE GREAT FORT OF THE PINES

*The Two Craigellachies – Aviemore – A disastrous fire – The charm
of Rothiemurchus – A signpost in the desert – Loch Morlich in
summertime – Loch-an-Eilean – A remarkable phenomenon – The
Shaws and the Cummings – The story of Alasdair Keir Shaw – The
bloody banquet – The crime of Alan Shaw – Iain Baold – The
Bodach-an-Doune – The Grants of Rothiemurchus – Patrick Mac-
Alpine Grant – Rob Roy to the rescue – MacAlpine as a justiciar –
The restless corpse – MacAlpine and Simon, Lord Lovat – MacAlpine's
wife claims her due.*

BETWEEN Alvie and Aviemore can be enjoyed one of the most
impressive views in the whole of Strathspey, with the forest of
Glenmore, like a great, green inland sea, cutting into the towering ramparts of the mountains. The mouth of the Larig Ghru,
or Stony Pass, separating Braeriach from the main massif of
Ben MacDuibh and the Cairngorm, can be seen with remarkable
clarity, but the obstruction offered by the upper Craigellachie
cuts off the prospect towards Kincardine.

The name "Craigellachie" comes from the Gaelic *Craig*, a
rock, and *ellachie*, alarm. There are two Craigellachies in Strathspey; the southern, or upper, one at Aviemore, and the northern,
or lower, in Banffshire, about forty miles downstream. The lower
Craigellachie marks the boundary of the strath, the River Spey
debouching from here out into the Moray lowlands.

As the name of these two "Rocks of Alarm" implies, they
were signal heights where beacons were lit to call the clan to
arms in times of danger; the Grant equivalent of the "Fiery
Cross"; and the fact that the name is duplicated in one contigu-
ous area is less cause for confusion than might be imagined,
because the upper is no more than a bare, uninhabited rock,
while the lower marks the site of a prosperous village with a
rail junction, distilling industry, and a brisk community life all
its own.

Aviemore, in the parish of Duthil, was originally in the possession of the Glenmoriston Grants and is now a charming little village, headquarters for ski-ers, mountaineers, and all those whose business or pleasure is to be found in association with the high places. Here the train from London turns away from Strathspey to complete the last stage of its journey to Inverness, but the railway station is also an important junction serving places to the north-east as far apart as Nairn and Aberdeen.

A disastrous fire in 1950 saw the destruction of the popular and comfortable Aviemore Hotel, together with the death of two guests. This conflagration was marked by several daring and gallant attempts at rescue, and one railway worker who, at great risk to himself, succeeded in saving some occupants from an upper floor window, was awarded the George Medal by H.M. the King.

For me, the chief feature of interest about Aviemore is the fact that it is the handiest means of approach to that part of Strathspey which, above all others, lays most claim to my affection and admiration; the lovely land of loch, mountain and forest called Rothiemurchus. I say "handiest" because I am one of these incurable reactionaries who still believe that a man's two legs are the most satisfying means of transport for all but prohibitive distances, and by taking the train from Cromdale to Aviemore I am able to start off fresh on a tramp otherwise beyond my compass within a single day.

I wonder if anyone has ever attempted to give a full and comprehensive description of Rothiemurchus? Many have certainly given fragmentary sketches relating to the place, and by imbibing all of these it is possible to gain some sort of impression of the whole; but an overall picture, describing the spiritual as well as the physical aspects of the surroundings is a task writers have apparently considered outwith their powers, and I am afraid I am no exception to this general rule.

All I know is that when I am crossing a crazy bridge over the Druie, devouring with my eyes the birch-clad slopes of the Ord Ban, or listening to my quiet remarks being flung back at me from the echoing walls of the water-encircled castle in Loch-an-Eilean, I am an entirely different being from what I am at other times.

For many years, during a fairly active life that has entailed living in several of the world's greatest cities and wandering extensively in the lesser-known parts of four continents, I harboured a nostalgic longing to live out the remainder of my days in Rothiemurchus; a yearning that was only allayed when I found my present ideal abode at Cromdale. But I can still appreciate the underlying reason for the signpost set up by a member of a Highland battalion in a lonely part of the Western Desert during the last war. This signpost had two arms. On one was written: "Divisional Command Post—2½ miles", and on the other, in bold lettering and pointing towards the north was the laconic direction: "ROTHIEMURCHUS—2,395 MILES".

The name Rothiemurchus is a corruption of the Gaelic *Rath-mor-ghiubhsaiche*, "Great Fort of the Pines", and is doubtless a reminder of very ancient days when "wailles", or strengths, made from large balks of timber, were erected as fortresses in thickly wooded areas. Lachlan Shaw, the Moray historian, describes it as lying "on the south-east side of the river, and, including Glenmore in Kincardine Parish, it maketh a semicircle, whereof the river is the diameter, and high mountains the circumference".

I doubt if anyone could give a better description of its location, even though this gives no clue when it comes to resolving a question that has always baffled me; namely, where Rothiemurchus ends and Glenmore begins. Not that I really want to know the answer, because I am sure the division is entirely manmade and I much prefer to look upon the two places as one— with perhaps Glen Eanaich thrown in.

Glenmore has been earmarked as a National Park, and a Youth Hostel has been opened at Glenmore Lodge on the eastern shore of Loch Morlich, on the most clearly defined track for beginning the long climb to the peak of Cairngorm. During the height of summer this eastern shore, with its fine stretch of sandy beach, offers a scene of much happy activity, with a camping site laid out to augment the accommodation at the Lodge, and much swimming, boating and sailing in progress; but in spring, autumn and winter it lapses into its more habitual solitude, when it is really difficult to imagine it ever being otherwise.

Some sensitive souls look with disapproval upon the crowds of young men in shorts and girls in slacks who are each summer discovering Loch Morlich in increasing numbers, but I cannot say that I agree with them. Although this is a very ancient land it is not at all allergic to youth and I, for one, can share in the joy of those young people who find here an unlooked-for heritage that is in itself infinitely more satisfying than the raucous seaside resorts and numerous holiday camps dotted everywhere along the coasts of the populous south. One fact, however, *has* saddened me. Last time I visited Morlich during the holiday season I heard more accents from Birmingham and the English Midlands than from the Lowland Scottish areas, and when I remarked upon this to a young Glaswegian holiday-maker, his reply was:

"Aye, I ken. I wanted two of my pals to come up here with me this year, but ye couldn't drag them away from Blackpool with a tractor. They say they're all out for a bit of life, and this place is dead."

Marvelling at a point of view that could see life in long rows of inanimate lamp-posts and nothing but death in the towering virility of skyward-reaching pines, I went sorrowfully on my way.

Rothiemurchus, for all its prevailing air of peace and quiet, has a past that was anything but tranquil. The earliest recorded landholders, the Comyns, or Cummings, were a far from amiable clan, and their Stewart successors, with the Wolf of Badenoch as their Chief, were more turbulent still. It was the Wolf who built the castle whose ruins are still a prominent feature on the little island in Loch-an-Eilean, and the strength of this can be appreciated when it is remembered that Grizel Mor, wife of a Grant Rothiemurchus laird, defended it successfully against MacDonell of Keppoch when he was retreating from the rout at Cromdale, even though the castle was then three hundred years old and had a garrison of but seven men.

Apart from the perfection of its scenic appeal, Loch-an-Eilean is worthy of attention for other reasons. For one thing, the island on which the castle ruins stand was almost certainly artificial in origin, a *crannog* of the type in use in Agricola's day, and was linked to the mainland by a submarine causeway, a good part of which is still in existence.

This underwater causeway, used for secret sorties when a besieging force had captured or destroyed the castle's boats, was said to have been a winding maze, the secret peregrinations of which were known to only three persons at any given time. So far, no one has thought of flying over the loch to take aerial photographs. These might show the windings of the causeway quite clearly. That it still exists is proved by the presence of leaf-bearing saplings growing straight out of the water without apparent land base of any kind.

One-time residents on the island in Loch-an-Eilean were the last ospreys to breed in Strathspey, but they have been gone a good many years now, and the castle's only remaining tenant is a most amazing echo. If you have never had the experience of having your voice recorded, and yet wonder how it must sound to ears other than your own, all that is necessary is to stand on the loch's western shore and give yourself a test in which the ruined castle wall takes the place of a microphone.

You may whisper, speak normally, or shout, the result is always instantaneous; back come your words in your natural voice every bit as clearly as you uttered them. Certain old writers (such as Lachlan Shaw) credit the island with returning a triple echo. This may have been possible when the castle was in a better state of preservation than it is now; or it may only be one more instance of the old chronicler's habit of "gilding the lily". If the latter, it was entirely unnecessary, for the present phenomenon is quite wonderful enough as it stands.

The Shaws, an off-shoot of the MacKintoshes of Clan Chattan, with the Wolf of Badenoch as their overlord, were noted in possession of Rothiemurchus as early as 1336, but it was more than a hundred years after that (1464) before a Shaw chief held the territory as a *right*, rather than as *duchus*. This was when the Bishop of Moray granted a charter in *feu ferme* to Alasdair Keir Shaw, son of the James Shaw who fell at the Battle of Harlaw.

This Alasdair Keir led a very eventful life. Shortly after his father's death, the Cummings decided this was an opportune moment to re-establish themselves in Rothiemurchus. By making a surprise attack on the leaderless Shaws, they succeeded in slaying a large number, but the young Chief, Alasdair Keir, then only a child, was saved by his nurse, who conveyed him to friends in Perthshire, in whose care she left him. When she returned home she found the whole of Rothiemurchus possessed by the Cummings, with all her kin either killed or fled, so she retired to an out-of-the-way cottage, where she sat down to her spinning and bided her time.

LOCH-AN-EILEAN. Echoing wall of Wolf of Badenoch's castle

NEAR
DULNAIN
BRIDGE.
Falls of
River
Dulnain
before
entering
Spey

Years went by, then late one night there came a knock at her door. Her heart gave a great leap. Could this be the visitation she had so long awaited, or was it some reiving Cumming envious of her small possessions? There was a quaver in her voice when she called softly, "Who is there?"

"It is I, your foster-son, Alasdair Keir," came the whispered reply.

Joy almost overcame the old nurse's caution, but not quite.

"It's the breath of that one I would know," she said. "Put your lips to the crack in the door above the latch if you would be recognized."

There was a murmur of men's voices outside, then one of them called that her order would be obeyed.

"No, no, that is not the breath of the little one I held to my breast," she moaned a second later.

"That was a foul jest!" snapped a man's voice. "Come to the door once more, mother, and you will know me."

Again the old woman came to the door, and this time she gave a cry of joy as she threw it wide to admit the young Chief of the Shaws and a dozen of his clansmen.

There was a night of feasting and rejoicing, the old nurse sacrificing her only cow for the entertainment of her guests. For three days the Shaws lay low in the lonely hill cottage while information was brought in about the movements of their enemies. Then, with plans carefully laid and reinforcements from Badenoch, the Shaws ambushed the Chief of the Cummings and a large party of his men in a hollow near Loch Pityoulish, where they slew them each and every one.

The place of this slaughter is still called Lag-na-Cuminich, "The Cummings' Hollow", and it is a strange fact that although birch and rowan abound in the immediate locality no tree has been known to grow in this hollow since the time of the killing.

After this the Cummings extended their feud against the Shaws to take in Clan Chattan as a whole. Alexander Cumming hanged ten young MacKintoshes near his Castle of Rait, and Malcolm MacKintosh retaliated by attacking the Castle of Nairn and slaying all the Cummings therein. At last, after a decisive battle in which they suffered a crushing defeat, the Cummings made overtures for peace, though still contemplating revenge. "Concealing their bloody purpose, they invited the leaders of

D

the MacKintoshes to the Castle of Rait, where all animosities were to be buried in the oblivion of the festive board; until a signal be given, when every Cumming at the table would bury his knife in the breast of a MacKintosh neighbour."

Fortunately for the MacKintoshes, a young man of their clan was the sweetheart of a young Cumming woman, and they had a meeting before this gory banquet was due to take place. The girl was bound by a clan oath of secrecy not to betray the intentions of her kin to an enemy, but knowing that her lover was waiting for her behind the Grey Stone near the Church of Croy, she confided words of warning to the stone, saying: "Woe to the MacKintosh who is not prepared when the head of the boar is carried in to the *Cuminich* feast."

Thus warned, the MacKintoshes did not await the arrival of the boar's head. Instead, they used their own pre-arranged signal, and it was Clan Chattan *sgians* that drank of Cummings' blood. There is good reason to believe that Alasdair Keir and his brother, Adam, as two warriors highly placed in the Clan Chattan councils, were present on this memorable occasion, and certain it is that no Cumming aspired for power in Strathspey from that time onward.

Mystery shrouds the facts that led up to the last Shaw laird being driven from Rothiemurchus. The author of *The Family of Dallas* says of the traditional story: "while it is impossible to reject this narrative as wholly apocryphal, it is equally impossible to bring it into accord with known fact."[1] Historical controversies are pesky things to get mixed up in, so I shall confine myself to presenting the generally accepted story, which is not without virtue in that it was believed implicitly by quite reputable writers who were much nearer in time and place to the happening it describes than the historians who nowadays try to disprove it.

The popular tale tells us that early in the sixteenth century the clan was left with a boy chief whose mother, a Campbell, married for her second husband Sir John Dallas of Cantry. The young chief's name was Alan, and he and his stepfather never hit it off from the start. Cut off from a sympathetic home life, young Alan devoted most of his time to the chase and his dogs. One day, when returning from the forest, his favourite hound

[1] *The History of Clan Shaw*, by Norman Shaw.

ran into the smiddy at Doune; only to be promptly kicked out
again by Dallas, who happened to be inside. That was the last
straw so far as the hot-headed Alan was concerned. Drawing
his dirk he rushed into the smiddy and slew his stepfather where
he stood, then, with the rage still in him, he haggled off the dead
man's head, took it home, and threw it at his mother's feet.

We have already said that Alan was young. Had he been
older he might have had a truer appreciation of his mother's
character, and foregone this last act of bravado. As it was, she
drove her son from her presence, and took immediate steps to
have him outlawed and disinherited, with the result that the
lands of Rothiemurchus were leased to Sir John, Laird of Grant,
who gave them to his son, Patrick Grant of Muckrach, "gin he
could hold them ".[1]

Young Alan Shaw had the sympathies of his clan, and after
being put to the horn he collected a band and set up in the full-
time employment of plundering his enemies. With a few more
years over his head he might have made quite a name for himself as a freebooter, but he was betrayed at Lag-na-Calrich by
MacKintosh of Strone, whom he mistook for a friend, was
arrested and conveyed to Castle Grant where, Lachlan Shaw tells
us: "he was civilly entertained, conveyed to his room at night,
and found dead in his chair next morning."

The Laird of Grant who gave Rothiemurchus to his second
son, Patrick, was known as *Iain Baold* (John the Simpleton), and
according to some authorities he was a man of weak intellect. If
that really was the case, then all I can say is he had a remarkable
record for one deemed a "natural". He held the chiefship for
forty-eight years, married twice, had issue by both marriages, was
a prominent member of the parliament that established the
Presbyterian Church in Scotland, was present at court when
Rizzio was murdered, and was greatly loved by his clansmen
who, on one occasion, promised to "support their Chief and
Maister against all invaders not only with their goods, but with
their bodies". He also amassed a fortune, and left his considerable estate even better than he found it.

Maybe the standards by which intellect was judged were
different in those days, but there is no doubt at all that the Grant
Chief showed remarkable shrewdness when he chose Patrick to

[1] Shaw MS. of 1758 at Moy Hall.

fill the role of laird at Rothiemurchus. Prior to his arrival the chief seat of previous lairds had been the Doune, a house perched upon an earthen hillock shaped like an upturned boat. There is every probability that this hillock was the site of the original Great Fort of the Pines that gave the district its name, but Patrick Grant was obviously not enamoured of it, and was soon building himself a new dwelling at the Dell.

Some say he took this step for purely strategic reasons, others that he was forced to do so because he could not stand the wailings of the *Bodach-an-Doune*, guardian spirit of the old Shaw dwelling, whose Gaelic lamentation could be heard at all sorts of odd hours. This never varied and, translated into English, it ran :

> " Ho, ho, ro, we go into captivity;
>   We go from lands and strongholds;
>   But though they have taken our country from us
>   We shall hope for the city of righteousness."

The Grant laird released this doleful spirit from his captivity by razing the old dwelling at Doune to the ground, while over his gateway at the Dell he placed the motto carved in stone that he had brought with him from his former castle at Muckrach. This read : " In God is al my traist, 1589 ", and has since been removed for a second time to the present house of Doune. This is built in pleasant parkland at some distance from the old hillock site, and is a sterling example of how a dwelling can mature and improve with age providing it is constantly lived in and regarded with the care associated with love rather than wild ambition.

From the time of that first Patrick, twelve Grant lairds have continued to hold the land in Rothiemurchus, and there have been some notable chieftains among them. Romantic sobriquets such as " The White Laird ", and the " Spreckled Laird ", would help to give us some idea of what these Grants looked like even if we had lacked the portraits of them, which are still in being, but the character who most grips our imagination was " Mac-Alpine ", fourth Laird, contemporary and friend of Rob Roy MacGregor.

The tales told about this real, old-time Highland laird are

legion, and have an added value in that many of them are vouched for historically. We also know exactly what he looked like. He was six feet five inches in height, of beautifully proportioned figure, golden-haired, blue-eyed, and extremely individual both in outlook and actions. He believed in giving his natural attributes all the enhancement a good tailor could provide, and we are told that his tartan trews were " laced down the sides with gold, the brogues on his beautifully formed feet were lined and trimmed with feathers; his hands, as soft and white as a lady's, and models as to shape, could draw blood from the finger-nails of any other hand he grasped, and they were so flexible they could be bent back to form a cup which would hold a table-spoonful of water ".[1]

Born in 1665, Patrick MacAlpine Grant, to give him his full name, was only twelve years old when he succeeded his father, and this at a time when the Shaws, supported by their Mac-Kintosh kinsmen in Badenoch, were far from resigned to the loss of their ancient home. When he was seventeen matters reached a head, and with the Clan Chattan men sending round the Fiery Cross, MacAlpine retaliated by dispatching a messenger in search of succour from the chief of the MacGregors at Aberfoyle.

The Shaws and Mackintoshes were massed all ready to strike when Rob Roy and his MacGregors arrived on the scene, and such was the fame of the celebrated freebooter that his presence was all that was needed to make the enemies of the Grant withdraw. When the hour came for departure, Rob Roy left behind two of his MacGregors who were noted as runners, and instructed MacAlpine to make use of them any time he found the need.

One of these MacGregors eloped with the beautiful *Mairi Bhuie*, Golden-haired Mary, a natural daughter of the Rothiemurchus laird, who strongly disapproved of the match at first, but was finally won over by his charming daughter. He gave her and her husband the croft at Alltdru, and their direct descendants farmed the land there up to seventy years ago.

The other MacGregor finally crossed over into Strathavon, and it was descendants of his who came over the hill into Cromdale, where they built a mill and started the distillery at Balmenach. Sir Robert Bruce Lockhart's mother was one of these MacGregors,

[1] *Memoirs of a Highland Lady*, by Elizabeth Grant of Rothiemurchus.

and he has much to say about this part of Strathspey in his book, *My Scottish Youth*.

Clan Chattan threats thus removed, MacAlpine gradually matured into the type of laird that was to give him his place in local history. Not content with the "tail" usually attendant upon a Highland chieftain, he also had his own private body-guard of twenty picked men under the command of *Ian Bain*, "Fair John", a Grant of Achnahatnich. By the time he was thirty he was a sort of Highland potentate, ruling not only his own territory of Rothiemurchus, but much of the neighbouring countryside as well.

A despot he undoubtedly was but, if all accounts be true, a just one. Backed by his trusty bodyguard he held court and was both judge and jury, dispensing justice with a finality against which there was no appeal. A man would be brought before him whom all the evidence proved to be a habitual criminal with no hope of reformation, another guilty of murder and robbery of the most despicable kind. In those days the only way to rid society of such threats was by imposition of the death sentence, and while MacAlpine did not boggle at this, he was still sufficiently fastidious to disapprove of the base instincts that could be roused by the spectacle of public executions. All he did was commit the prisoner to the attentions of his bodyguard, and thereafter he would quietly disappear. A few weeks later, perhaps, his body would be found lying in the underbrush with a *sgian* in his heart, or swinging from the limb of a tree deep in the forest. In each case the carcass would carry a mark denoting execution by order of MacAlpine, and in no known instance was his justice ever questioned, which is more than can be said of the judgments passed by the majority of the Baillie Barons, who were chiefly responsible for the maintenance of the law in those days.

During an affray between the Shaws and some of MacAlpine's bodyguard, the Chief of the former was slain, and the Grant laird refused permission for him to be buried in Rothiemurchus kirkyard. As this had been the burial ground of the Shaws for centuries, they ignored MacAlpine's ban and laid their Chief to rest with full clan honours. But MacAlpine was not so easily flouted. Next morning when Mrs. Shaw of Dalnavert opened her door in response to a knock, the body of her dead husband fell into her arms.

Again Shaw was buried, and again he made an inexplicable resurrection, and so for several weeks the merry game went on. At length MacAlpine appeared to relent. He gave permission for Shaw to be buried inside the kirk, instead of the kirkyard. Greatly mollified, the Shaws accepted this as a special mark of respect, and one can well imagine their chagrin when they found that the Grant had moved his pew so that he sat directly over his old enemy where, on cold Sunday mornings, he could warm his feet and indulge his disdain at the same time by stamping on the dead man's face.

The notorious Simon Fraser, Lord Lovat, has long been hailed as the epitome of all that was individualistic in the old type of Highland chief, but the only thing he had that MacAlpine Grant lacked was a natural bent towards deceit and double-dealing. When it is recalled that those two, as in the case of Rob Roy, were contemporary and actually met on several occasions, one can well imagine the joy it must have been when they ran foul of each other.

When Lovat married Margaret, fourth daughter of Sir Ludovick, Laird of Grant, in 1717, it was an occasion for much celebration and merry-making in Strathspey, and when the Fraser left for home with his bride, MacAlpine and his bodyguard were among the gentlemen of Grant who accompanied them. At Castle Dounie, the Fraser seat, the feasting was continued, and when the Strathspey men took the floor to dance, their more northerly hosts were left gasping their amazement. Never before had they seen men dance with such verve and grace, and a bard even wrote a song to commemorate the event. Translated from the Gaelic this ran:

> "There was one they styled 'the Tulloch',
>   Mullochard, and yet another,
>   To trip with these matchless three,
>   Where could you find another."

On the following morning a sarcastic remark from MacAlpine put an end to an old Highland custom. This was when an attendant came and asked him to subscribe to a collection for the bride.

"Had *my* daughter married my cattleman, I would have kept

her from begging for at least seven years," he said dryly, as he tossed the man a coin. The *Baidse*, as it was called, was discontinued from that day.

Two years later the Laird of Rothiemurchus was again at Castle Dounie to celebrate the birth of Lady Lovat's son, and her husband chose the occasion to practise one of his childish jokes. MacAlpine was invited to cut open a pie, and when he did so a pigeon flew out, so startling him that he threw up a hand to protect his head.

"MacAlpine has scrogged his bonnet!" shouted Lovat in high glee.

"If so, a double-dealing traitor shall scrog opposite him," retorted MacAlpine coldly, swiftly drawing his sword and wiping all sign of mirth from his host's face.

Lovat, ever more noted for discretion than valour, was quick to apologize, but the incident reveals clearly the outstanding difference between the two men. They had another encounter when playing cards at Castle Grant.

"Why the devil don't you play?" snapped Lovat impatiently.

"I do aver that this hand would suit you better than it does me," replied MacAlpine, affecting to be sorely puzzled.

"Why so?"

"Just look," invited MacAlpine, exposing his hand, "a knave between two kings."

MacAlpine strongly disliked lawyers and doctors, but got on reasonably well with parsons; at least to the extent of tolerating them. One day while out walking with the minister of Duthil, the latter stumbled.

"God and Mary be with you," said MacAlpine, steadying him by the arm.

"God with *me*, Mary with *you*," retorted the Calvinistic prelate. "What better was she than my own mother?"

"Of the mothers I really know very little," said the Laird quietly, "but I'll admit to a very great difference in the sons."

MacAlpine was married twice; first to Mary Grant, daughter of Patrick, Tutor of Grant, and secondly, to Rachel Grant of Tullochgorm. He was seventy when he married Rachel, then a very young girl, and the manner of his courting is worth telling.

"I hear you have fine daughters, and I have come to look at

them with a view to marriage," he said to Grant of Tullochgorm.
" May I be introduced to them one at a time? "

When the eldest daughter was brought to him he asked her
what she would do if she had a tocher as big as Craigowrie.
With jewels and finery awaiting purchase somewhere, she gave
him the impression that it would not last long. Repeating the
question to two other daughters, the would-be suitor got the
same reply.

" And is that all the lassies you have? " he asked Tullochgorm.

" No, I've one more, my youngest," was the answer. " You'll
see her when she comes in with the cows."

In due course the young Rachel arrived and was asked the
same question.

" A wedding tocher, no matter how big it be, would be of little
worry to me," she answered frankly. " It would only come my
way if I were wed, and I'm sure my husband could advise me
how to use it wisely."

This reply delighted MacAlpine, and very soon after Rachel
became his bride. It was for her he built the earliest version
of the present house of Doune. His two wives bore him eight
sons and a daughter; the last-named and five of the sons being
Rachel's contribution.

It must have appeared as if MacAlpine was well-nigh indestruc-
tible, so hale and hearty was he in his old age. But even if he
did not have an Achilles' heel, he had a big toe which proved his
downfall. An injury to this was neglected, it went septic, and
finally killed him in 1743, when he was in his eighty-fourth year.

He was succeeded by James " The Spreckled Laird ", who,
with his wife, did not treat his stepmother or her offspring with
all the fairness she expected. One day, feeling herself slighted
in church, the forthright Rachel lost all restraint. Going out
into the kirkyard she ran to MacAlpine's grave, pulled off her
shoe, and using its heel as a knocker started thumping on her
husband's tombstone, at the same time shouting aloud:

" MacAlpine, MacAlpine, dinna lie dozzening there, but come
back here for yae short half-hour to see me richted."

Another notable tomb in the churchyard at Rothiemurchus
is that of Fearchar Shaw, *Corfhiaclach* (The buck-toothed), sole
survivor of the Clan Ay after the Clan Battle on the North Inch
at Perth, in 1396. He died in 1405, and the *bodach* displaced

from its old home at Doune has long assumed new duties by acting as guardian of his sepulchre. This consists of a flat slab of rock, bearing an inscription of identification and weighted down by five stones looking very much like petrified sawn logs. Four of these are placed one at each corner of the gravestone, a fifth in the middle, and the *bodach* is said to assure the early death of any persons foolhardy enough to remove them.

Only three men are known to have attempted this sacrilege, and all of them died within a year of their vandalism. One of these was a footman of the Duke of Bedford, who rented Doune House as a summer residence. He took away one of the stones and threw it in the river, but was forced by his master to retrieve it and put it back again. Three days later he was drowned while attempting to ford the Spey.

THE MAGIC OF GLENMORE

THE road from Rothiemurchus to Glenmore passes through the hamlet of Coylum Bridge. This takes its name from the Gaelic Coimh-leum, meaning "a leaping together"; referring to the junction of the Luinag and the Bennie some distance above the bridge.

To come suddenly upon Coylum in the height of summer, with bridge and stream shaded from the searching sun by a canopy of deciduous leaves, is to feel a nostalgic tightening of the heart-strings; so divinely peaceful and satisfying is the scene. It is also utterly unexpected in surroundings where the wild grandeur of the rearing pine is the norm, rather than the pastoral spread of beech and elm.

There is, in fact, an air of unbelievable rural bliss about this place, intensified by the riot of garden flowers embellishing the small general store and post office situated close to the bridge. The blaze of colour this provides forms the perfect background to the dappled greenery through which it is viewed.

Go there on a summer evening when tree and hill are begin-ning to cast long shadows, and lean on the bridge's stone parapet gazing down at the broiling waters below. A light wind may stir the leaves overhead, causing shadows to flit about, and through them you may see Coylum's particular sprite, the *Bodach Cleocain Dearg*, or Old Man in the little Red Cloak, leaping nimbly from boulder to boulder as he did in the days before the bridge was built; for his especial duty was to guide travellers across the chasm.

Beyond Coylum the scene quickly changes. The metalled highway is left behind for a track winding over the open moorland whose only mantle is heather or the white skeletons of barkless and isolated dead trees. Beyond this again, the path mounts upward in ever-widening sweeps until at last it enters the cover of the trees; and from this point one's journeyings in the Forest of Glenmore have begun.

There are two commonly used entrances to the Great Glen. From Abernethy it is reached by the pass of Revoan, the track passing within feet of the remarkable Green Loch, while from Kincardine the approach is by the Sluggan of Eas, or Throat of the Waterfall, an impressive, thickly-wooded ravine, more than two miles long.

Glenmore lies in the parish of Kincardine; no doubt because an old-time prelate in the Lowland city of Elgin thought in terms of mileage rather than natural features when parish boundaries were being defined. Those people who speak loudly against centralization of administration, whereby Lowlanders are still entrusted with the management of Highland affairs, would do well to note this piece of bureaucratic ineptitude, because it will prove to them that the ills they contend against are not of recent origin.

Lonely and detached, its chief asset an overpowering grandeur, Glenmore, with its sparse population, could not have greatly increased Kincardine's income by the payment of parish dues, but it has made its inclusion worth while in another way because, with the peak of the Cairngorm as its south-eastern limit, Kincardine can claim the distinction of having the loftiest parish-boundary in Britain; one that is over 4,000 feet high.

The fact that the old "Thieves' Road" traversed the whole length of the glen is in itself proof of its wild and thinly-inhabited aspect. It is, therefore, all the more amusing to see how an Edinburgh servant of the Crown described the place when the lands were being granted (after a resignation by Sir George Mac-Kenzie of Rosehaugh) to the Duke of Gordon.

" And this to include the Forest and Woods of Glenmore, Hills and Glens belonging thereto, with castles, towers, fortalices, manor places, houses, biggings, yards, orchards, parks, shielings, grassings, outsets, insets, tofts, crofts, parts, pendicles and pertinents thereof."

I suppose the scrivener who got out that masterpiece must have been hypnotized by the acreage and could only think in terms of the Lothians or Lanarkshire. I particularly like his reference to "orchards". Considering the lowest part of Glenmore lies at an altitude of over 1,000 feet, with morning and night frosts liable to occur in ten months out of twelve, getting an orchard's blossoms to fruit would be quite an undertaking.

The first historical mention we have of Glenmore is as a Royal Forest, but we know beyond shadow of doubt that it was the hunting ground of the Stewart Barons of Kincardine, descendants of the Wolf of Badenoch, at a much earlier time.

Robin Og Stewart, of the Kincardine family, was greatly famed as a hunter. He was also well versed in the etiquette recognized by the *Daoine Sith*, or fairies. Once when returning from the chase he had occasion to pass the *sithean*, or fairy hill, of Domhnall Mor, King of the Fairies, on the western shore of Loch Morlich, and heard the silver drones of the Little Folk piping their sovereign home. Deciding this was as good a time as any for obtaining a fairy gift, *and* knowing the correct procedure, he snatched off his bonnet and threw it towards the sounds of the music, crying out: "*Is leatsa so, is leatsa sin*" (this is yours and that is mine).

The fairy musician immediately dropped his tiny silver pipes and vanished. Greatly thrilled at winning such a prize, Robin Og tucked the spoils under his plaid and ran all the way home, but when he arrived there and went to show his treasure all his eager hand brought forth was a bent blade of grass and a puffball.

Another day Robin Og was hunting in Glenmore when he dropped a hind with his short bow and laid his *sgian-dubh* down on the grass beside his kill, preparatory to gralloching. When, however, he went to pick up his knife again it had vanished. He made a fruitless search for it, then took the *sgian* from his dirk and laid that down beside him. It also disappeared. Drawing his dirk, and being careful not to let it out of his hand, he finished the job as best he could and, with the deer slung from his shoulder, set off towards home. He had reached the stretch of sand at Loch Morlich, now so well-known to holiday-makers, when he was stopped by an old man wearing a grey plaid. The stranger held one hand tucked inside his plaid, but the other, a blood-dripping red, was fully exposed.

This time Young Robin knew that ordinary fairy etiquette would be of no avail; for he recognized the old man before him as the *Lamh Dearg*, "The Spectre of the Bloody Hand".

"So it is Robin Og, is it?" said the spectre. "And carrying one of my poor slaughtered innocents, I see."

"I killed it but an hour ago in Glacan-beadaich" (Broom Hollow), said Robin boldly.

"You may call it *Glacan-beadaich*, but I call it *Glacan-bealaidh*," retorted the spectre; thereby punning on the name so that *beadaich* (broom) was replaced by *bealaidh* (impudence). "Here are your two missing knives. I removed them to put a check to your slayings. Be more sober in future when you come hunting in Glenmore."

Dr. Forsyth says: "The Red hand was evidently a true Celt. Love of nature, fondness for animals, passionate attachment to home . . . are sentiments that still run in the blood of every Highlander, and will live in him till his heart grows cold."

These Stewarts of Kincardine and Glenmore were an outstanding race, and no book on Strathspey can afford to dismiss them with only a passing reference. Ancient barons in their district, and of royal descent in direct line from King Robert II, one branch of the family were also the appointed foresters of Glenmore.

The first man to hold this post was Lieutenant Robert Stewart, a subaltern under Captain Robert Campbell of Glenlyon, whose name is still execrated as the treacherous murderer of Glencoe. When orders for the massacre arrived Robert Stewart refused to have any part in it. He was coaxed, threatened and importuned, but stood firm by his decision, even though this meant having to resign his commission and ultimately flee as a refugee to the north. The Duke of Gordon gave him sanctuary, and being unable to get him reinstated in the Army, bestowed upon him the appointment of Keeper of the Forest of Glenmore, in those days a lucrative post of considerable advantage.

Robert Stewart married in Glenmore and had a large family. He lived for more than a hundred years, and his eldest son, James, prospered to such an extent by thrift and industry that his neighbours gave ready credence to a fanciful story whereby his good fortune was attributed to his having found a hidden treasure. James also lived to a great age. When he was ninety-three he was noted in the Old Statistical Account as a "blooming, correct, sensible man, and comes to church the coldest day in winter". He died from a fall when crossing the ice-covered Alltmore on Christmas Day, 1795.

John Stewart of Pityoulish, who was said to resemble his grandfather, who was the third most impressive figure in the North Highlands, was in his day rated the finest-looking man in Strathspey. In 1797 Sir James Grant of Grant appointed him a Deputy Lieutenant of Inverness-shire, an honour rarely conferred on any other than landed proprietors. He was present at Kinrara on the occasion of the great reception given by the Marquis of Huntly to Prince Leopold, and when Huntly introduced him to the Prince as "an old rebel", he retorted: "How could I be otherwise, seeing I've always been your lordship's faithful servant?"

One of the English guests at this reception was very ambitious to bag a Glenmore stag, and confided this wish to his host.

"You'd better see Pityoulish as to that," smiled the Marquis. "His permission is much more important than mine."

"Nevertheless, if I have yours I shall be well satisfied," was the arrogant response.

"Please yourself," shrugged Huntly. "But I'll be surprised if you don't repent it."

Next morning the guest went out with his gun, and was duly detected by Pityoulish through his spyglass. Before the hunter had covered a mile he found himself confronted by the Keeper of the Forest, who immediately asked him what he intended to do with his gun.

"What is that to you?" snapped the guest haughtily. "I come from Kinrara."

"Then no doubt you'll have a letter from his lordship?" said Pityoulish.

"I find a gun of more use than letters when I go hunting," was the sneering retort.

"In that case, you've no right to be here," said Pityoulish. "I'll trouble you to hand over your gun."

The would-be hunter, somewhat vain of his bodily strength and never dreaming but that he could prove more than a match for one of Pityoulish's advanced years, scornfully ignored this demand. Next thing he knew he was flat on his back; the Keeper of the Forest walking off with the offending weapon tucked under his arm. Later, when the outraged sportsman complained to his host, insult was added to injury, for Huntly only laughed and told him he had been forewarned.

John Stewart of Pityoulish was forthright in all things; even his wooing. He fell in love with the charming Mary Grant of Kinchirdy, but her father left him in no doubt that he preferred a rival suitor in the person of the minister of Abernethy. One day this rival had been preaching at Kincardine and seized the opportunity to spend the night at Kinchirdy. It was summer, with dawn breaking at a very early hour. Hearing a commotion outside about three a.m., the minister went to the window and looked out. A joyous, laughing procession was making its way down to the Spey. When this had been reached, he saw Pityoulish and his brother join hands to make a "king's chair" for the lovely Mary. Seated in this she was carried across the river dry-shod. Stewart had removed his lady-love from under his rival's nose and, the minister at Duthil being a party to his plans, the couple were married without delay.

Captain John Stewart, son of Pityoulish's brother, Charles, was known as the *oichear mor*, or big officer. He was far and away the strongest man in Strathspey. At Auchernach were two round boulders called *clachan neart*, or "stones of strength", and only one man in ten could lift the smaller of these on to the top of the adjoining stone dyke. No man in the district, however, other than Captain Stewart, could do this with the larger; and his strength did not stop there. One day he placed the boulders one on top of the other, picked them both up, and tossed them over the wall with apparent ease.

But the greatest of all the redoubtable Stewart band was John Roy Stewart, soldier, bard, and Gay Galliard of "the '45". His story is indeed worth remembering, and even though it has been told before can bear repetition.

John Roy was the son of Donald, grandson of the last Baron of Kincardine. His mother, a Shaw of Rothiemurchus, was his father's second wife, and she bore her red-headed son when she was fifty-three years old. That was in 1700. He received an education somewhat better than his native strath could afford,

DESOLATE LOCH AVON. Source of the River Avon below Cairngorm

A RARELY VISITED
LOCH

Evening at
lonely Loch
Achnuic

even studying in France and Portugal, and his position in society was assured when he obtained a commission in the Royal Scots Greys.

When the Black Watch was raised John Roy decided the kilt was more to his liking than jackboot and spur, but his application for a commission in the Highland Company was refused. He felt this rebuff so keenly that he resigned from the Army, and during the next few years the only glimpses we have of him are as roysterer and associate of Jacobites. This mode of life ultimately landed him in Inverness jail, but from this he escaped.

A reference to his imprisonment was made during the trial of Simon Fraser, Lord Lovat, with whom John Roy had long been on intimate terms. Lovat was asked if he could remember the year in which John Roy Stewart broke out of Inverness jail, and his lordship replied: "In 1740." Later Lovat was forced to admit that he himself had been Sheriff of Inverness at that time, and the inference that he had connived in the prisoner's escape was greatly strengthened when a witness swore that John Roy had stayed at Lovat's house for six weeks after regaining his freedom.

This witness, a man named Chevis, was next asked how Lord Lovat and John Roy Stewart had diverted themselves during this stay. He answered that they used much of their time in composing verses in the Erse tongue, whose main gist was that when Young Charlie came over there would be blood and blows.

The purpose of this questioning was to prove that Lovat consorted with rebels, and in furtherance of this a second witness, John Gray of Rogart, was called. He was asked if he knew John Stewart, "commonly called Roy", and replied that he had been acquainted with him when he was Lieutenant Quartermaster in the Dragoons, and later saw him with the rebels in Stirling. He described him as being always very gaily dressed, varying his costume from the kilt to the garb of the Lowlands.

The prosecution had, of course, little difficulty in proving that John Roy was a rebel of the most active variety. He had been seen in Boulogne when on his way to visit the Pretender in Rome, and had fought against the British at Fontenoy on May 11th, 1745. On the night before this battle he had crossed the lines to the British camp and enjoyed a happy reunion with Lewis Grant of Auchterblair and other friends from Strathspey

E

who were serving with the Black Watch. Next day they met in bloody strife, and it is well to remember that it was the great fighting retreat of the Black Watch on this occasion that saved the defeated British Army from annihilation.

John Roy was still in France when he heard that the White Banner of the Stewarts had been raised at Glenfinnan on the 19th August, 1745, and within the month he joined his Prince at Blair Athole. Being well known during his Army days in Edinburgh, he went there and raised a body of troops which he called "The Edinburgh Regiment". Although polyglot in its personnel, the battalion had a good hard core of Highlanders from Perthshire and Strathspey, and acquitted itself with great honour in its first big battle at Prestonpans.

In passing I must mention another Strathspey man who was with John Roy on this occasion; Colquhoun Grant of Burnside, who came from my own parish of Cromdale. Towards the close of the battle, when the British cavalry were breaking and about to flee, Grant knocked an English officer out of his saddle and jumped on his horse's back. He then charged a squadron of dragoons, who turned tail and set off for Edinburgh as fast as they could go. When the city was reached, people in the High Street were treated to the unusual spectacle of a large body of Dragoons thundering along towards the castle pursued by a solitary, kilted man on horseback. The incident ended with the regular cavalry reaching safety within the castle walls and Grant showing his disgust by defiantly sticking his dirk into the castle gate before retiring unscathed. This same Grant later settled in Edinburgh as a respectable Writer to the Signet.

But, to return to John Roy.

At the Battle of Falkirk he found himself opposite his old regiment, the Scots Greys.

"Ho, there you are, we shall soon be with you," shouted his former Commanding Officer, Colonel Whitney, in recognition.

"And it's the warm welcome you'll receive," called back John Roy.

He had barely spoken when Colonel Whitney, struck by a chance shot, fell dead from the saddle.

During the long retreat from Derby, John Roy's name is continuously mentioned in the daily orders of the Jacobite Army as a commander of rearguards and "petronils". It was his shouts of "claymore, claymore!" that struck terror into the hearts of Cumberland's men at Clifton. Later, when an attempt was made to surprise him at Strathbogie, he first retired to Fochabers and then struck back with a night attack, cutting off a party of Campbells and cavalry.

At the head of his Edinburgh Regiment he was in the forefront of the battle at Culloden, and one of Cumberland's captain's said: "If all the Highlanders had fought as well as the officer with the red head and small hand, the issue might have been different."

John Roy was almost broken-hearted after Culloden, and he tells us something of his grief in his verses "Lament for the Brave fallen on Drummossie Moor". He attributed the defeat to the absence of the MacPhersons (it is a remarkable fact that the Jacobites never lost a battle when the MacPhersons were present under the leadership of Cluny, their Chief) and the fierce, blinding storm that blew in the faces of the clansmen.

After Culloden he was outlawed and a large reward offered for his capture, but, like his master, though often in great peril he was never betrayed. He sought refuge in his beloved Glenmore, and the cave which bears his name can still be seen high up on the face of Craig-odhrie, near the Green Loch.

His adventures as a fugitive were many. Once a boy, named Peter Bell, came upon a party of soldiers when he knew the unsuspecting John Roy was bathing his feet in a stream little more than a hundred yards away. The boy established friendly relations with the soldiers and cajoled them into letting him exhibit his prowess as a drummer by beating a tattoo.

John Roy, sitting out of view behind a clump of trees, heard the drum beat out a warning to which words in Gaelic had been supplied. In English these would be:

> "Flee, and linger not,
>   Away, away!
>   Come not again to-night,
>   For pursuers are near;
>   Come not again to-night,
>   Away, away!"

"I know not what drum that is, but the *beat* is Peter Bell's, for it was myself taught him that tattoo," said John Roy as he stole quietly away.

That night he was practising a new form of concealment, the anonymity that comes from mingling with a crowd, for he joined in the festivities of a wedding at Balnagowan, Nethyside. More than eighty years afterwards an old lady in Grantown, Marjorie Stewart, was still boasting that she danced that night with John Roy. She died in 1826 at the age of 101.

At last the hunt for John Roy became so intense that he no longer found it safe to shelter under any man's roof. Forced to take entirely to the wild, he lived for a time in a gorge at Connage, over the hill from Bad-an-Aodinn. The smooth slab of stone he sheltered under can still be seen there. A little girl who brought his food daily was his only link with the outer world, and to her he used to sing his own paraphrase of the twenty-third Psalm:

> "The Lord's my targe, I will be stout,
>   With dirk and trusty blade,
>   Though Campbells come in flocks about,
>   I shall not be afraid.
>
> Though they mow down both corn and grass,
>   Nay, seek me underground;
>   Though hundreds guard each road and pass,
>   John Roy shall not be found."

It was while here that he heard tidings of the Prince, also a fugitive. Prince Charlie had a great affection for John Roy, whom he always referred to as " the body ", and full significance of the ties binding John Roy to his master can be appreciated by noting the manner of their meeting in this time of great peril.

The Prince was hiding in a cave in Badenoch, and when he saw his trusty follower approaching he mischievously decided to startle him. John Roy was negotiating a puddle at the entrance to the cave, and paying but little attention to a man lying by the wall under cover of a plaid, when the latter jumped suddenly erect and exposed his face to view. Indescribable joy leapt into John Roy's eyes.

"Good lord, it's my dear master himself! " he cried, and such was his emotion that he slumped to the ground in a dead faint.

John Roy remained with his royal master and accompanied him to France. He died in exile when he was fifty-two.

John Roy Stewart was not the only man from Glenmore forced by his actions to go into exile. John MacGibbon of Tontiri (a Cumming) was another, and there is a pathos about his story that I have always found most poignantly appealing.

MacGibbon and John Grant of Richailleach were neighbouring farmers who, unfortunately, could not get on together. MacGibbon was repairing a fence when Grant's son appeared and began abusing him over some matter concerning sheep. Mac-Gibbon had a gun lying nearby for the purpose of scaring crows. He picked this up, telling the young Grant that if he did not go off his land, and stay off, he would shoot him.

The only effect this had was to produce a fresh torrent of abuse and insults. Provoked beyond endurance, MacGibbon raised the gun and fired. He afterwards confided in a letter to a friend that he had not intended to hit the young man, but merely to frighten him. Alas, the shot took effect, blowing a great hole in young Grant's thigh. MacGibbon tried to stanch the wound then, finding this hopeless, decided to disappear.

When the dead body was found there was a great hue and cry for the killer, but he was never apprehended. He hid for a time in a hole under a tree in the Doire-gharbh (rough hollow) near Loch Garten, then managed to get out of the country.

It is the sequel to this story that I find so moving. About thirty years after this tragedy a young man, named John Mac-Queen, serving with Marlborough's army in Holland, left his camp one evening for a stroll. He had paused to watch some labourers building an embankment when one of them, an old man, straightened his toil-bent back and smiled, his eyes lighting up at sight of the tartan. Then, to MacQueen's amazement, the old man addressed him in Gaelic.

"Where do you come from?" he asked.

"Scotland," was MacQueen's reply.

"I'm knowing that," said the old man. "Which part?"

"Strathspey," said MacQueen.

"And whereabouts in Strathspey?"

"Glenmore, in Kincardine."

A mist of tears showed in the old man's eyes.

"Tell me, are there still rowan trees at Buchonich?" he asked with trembling voice.

"Yes, the rowans are standing there still," nodded the younger man.

It was later discovered that this poor old labourer was the fugitive MacGibbon of Tontiri, and the degree of his punishment will be readily understood when it is remembered that it was the trees of his native land he inquired after, rather than its people. For a man who loved the natural beauty of his country like that, exile must have been doubly cruel.

A cairn now stands at Richailleach to mark the spot where young Grant fell, and this is only one of a vast number in the parish of Kincardine. Hundreds are visible on hill and moorland, while countless others are hidden deep in the woodlands. Some have been built in comparatively recent times as path-guides, landmarks or works of commemoration, but by far the greater number are prehistoric in origin.

In the latter class the Carn-na-feola (Cairn of the Flesh), situated on the moorland near the Mill of Kincardine, is perhaps the most notable. It is rendered distinctive from other, smaller cairns surrounding it in that it is ringed by a rampart of earth. In the central great heap of rocks, a stone cist was found about a hundred years ago. It was four feet square and covered by a flagstone. It contained the remains of a man, woman and child, and the skulls were in a perfect state of preservation. As has so often happened, however, these relics fell into ignorant hands and quickly disappeared.

A cairn of more modern origin is Archie's Cairn at Glaic Bothan, below the Eagle's Cliff on Cairngorm. This commemorates a tragedy that took place towards the beginning of the nineteenth century, when two young men, William (nicknamed "Foxie") Fraser and Archie Fyfe, of Sleighich, went out in moonlight to try to shoot a fox as it left its den. Somehow Fyfe dropped his gun on a slope and, when trying to retrieve it, it went off, mortally wounding him. He lived long enough to declare it was a pure accident, with no blame attaching to his companion, but, remembering that they were both in love with the same girl, many put this down to his Christian charity, and it is significant that Fraser left the country shortly afterwards.

While out tramping with a friend one day we fell to discussing this matter of cairns. His view was that they represented a remarkable expense of energy, out of all proportion to the results obtained. We were right in the heart of the wildly beautiful Mondadh Ruidh country, and he had a plentiful selection of examples on which to base his remarks.

"I'm not referring to the useful cairns, such as those raised to mark the track when the snows of winter come," he explained. "What I'm really getting at are those carefully-built piles of stones dotted all over the place to commemorate something or other."

"And very durable memorials they've been," I said.

"Yes, but of what?" he demanded. "No one I ask ever seems to know. All the satisfaction I get is the knowledge that a whole host of stories are lying there under my nose and I'll never learn a thing about them. For a man in my line, that is particularly infuriating."

My friend was Fiction Editor of a chain of newspapers, and I could sympathize with him, because I had experienced similar feelings many a time.

"Just look at that cairn over there," he went on. "From its position it can't be a landmark or guide, so it was obviously put there to commemorate somebody or something. But can you, or anyone else nowadays, tell me what?"

We were at that moment near the junction of the Glasalt and the Uisge-dubh-pullchoin, and it so happened that in this particular instance I *could* satisfy his curiosity. I explained it was a memorial to one of the soldiers who perished in a storm in 1804 when trying to negotiate the Larig Ghru. The tragic story was unknown to him, so I had to describe the occurrence in full.

It involved seven militiamen who left their barracks in Edinburgh to spend a Christmas furlough in Strathspey. When they got to Castleton, near Braemar, there was heavy snow on the hills, with promise of more to come, and they were advised to stay where they were until the sky cleared a bit. But a soldier with a pass in his pocket and his home within striking distance is an impatient creature, and all attempts at dissuasion were in vain.

Shortly after the travellers left Castleton snow began to fall, and by the time they got into Strath Avon they were battling through a furious blizzard. Anyone who knows the route they had to follow, even under the most favourable conditions, must shudder at the thought of the task they were setting themselves, but it is to be remembered that these were hardy, native sons of the country, and they pushed resolutely on.

When they reached Lochan-a-bhainne they were unable to see more than a couple of feet ahead, and here it was that they took a wrong turning. Not only that, they began to lose touch with each other. One of the party, William Forsyth, managed to maintain contact with his brother, Alexander, and when the latter fell unconscious he picked him up and carried him. The rest revived Alexander, so that he was able to regain his feet after a while and make his way on alone. He survived the dreadful journey, but the brother who had expended his strength to save him perished.

One other man, Donald Elder, succeeded in getting over the hills with Alexander Forsyth, and together they found shelter at the Drum. All the others, William Forsyth, Donald Cameron, John Tulloch, Peter MacKenzie and Donald Ross, sank into the snow, never to rise again.

It was eighteen months after the event before the body of Peter MacKenzie was discovered, and this under such gruesome circumstances that the finder, a man named Cameron, never recovered from the shock.

"The body of John Tulloch was found close to this spot where we are now standing," I said to my friend. "It is to perpetuate his memory that the cairn you have just drawn attention to was raised."

CHAPTER VI

MOUNTAINS, GEMS AND ABOMINABLE SNOWMEN

The Pass of Revoan – A strange cemetery – A swim in the Green Loch – Climbing the Cairngorm – The Marquis's Well – James Grant strikes it rich – The Old Woman of the Stone – The great beryl – The Shelter Stone – A day on the high levels – The spectre of Ben MacDuibh – What Dr. Kellas saw – The experience of Dr. Collie – Mysterious tracks in Strathspey – A Canadian experience – The Bodach Mor explained.

THE three routes already described as being the best approaches to Glenmore are of equal value when the intention is to climb Cairngorm. I like best that which comes up from Nethyside via Forest Lodge and the Pass of Revoan (Rebhoan) to the defile skirting Loch-an-Uaine, the Green Loch.

On this route one encounters the nearest likeness to a "Tres-pass" sign in the whole of Strathspey; a notice near Forest Lodge to the effect that motor vehicles are not permitted to travel beyond this point. I am not quite clear as to the reason for this ban, but I must confess I am very much in accord with it, because the invasion of engine exhausts in such surroundings, except in cases of extreme necessity, could only approximate to sacrilege of the grossest kind.

Beyond Forest Lodge, when the trees are left behind and the road mounts above the moss towards the Pass of Revoan, a slight divergence will bring one to what is surely one of the strangest cemeteries in Britain. Here cairns mark the last resting place of favourite horses, and miniature tombstones those of equally well-loved dogs. The dogs are all coffined, I understand, and many of them have been brought great distances so that, like their masters, they could be interred in the land of their fathers. I know not who initiated this custom, but it has obviously continued over a lengthy period, and I consider the practice singularly attractive.

At one time there was a fair number of steadings along this

route, but nowadays the only sign of man-made habitation is the keeper's cottage at Revoan, and a bothy farther down the pass where the stormbound or benighted traveller can find shelter or rest. A few hundred yards from the bothy lies the Green Loch.

If I tried for a month of Sundays I could never even begin to describe adequately the effect the Green Loch has always had upon me; and this not merely because of the amazing colour of its water.

Its unlooked for situation may have something to do with this, because, somehow or other, with Creag Loisgte at no great distance on the one hand, and Creag-nan-Gall rearing abruptly upwards from the water's edge on the other, a loch in any shape or form is just about the last thing one would expect to find.

So far as I know, no indisputable explanation for the startling green of the water has ever been forthcoming, although old-time residents in Glenmore had a ready explanation for this phenomenon. It was caused by the fairies using the loch as a laundry to wash their green cloaks. Unfortunately, this could never be definitely proved, for if an observer were to catch sight of a naked fairy shoulder gleaming in the moonlight total blindness would be the result, and this was too great a risk to run. In any case, why go to such trouble to prove something that everyone already knew to be true?

I had heard so much about the Green Loch that I did not feel at all like a stranger when I visited it for the first time. Along the shallow south and western shores I could see short, fragile grass growing on the loch bottom, and noted the trunks of fallen trees with bare, spear-like branches showing clearly in the transparent water. These trees, inert relics of the ancient Caledonian forest, have probably been immersed thus for upwards of 2,000 years, and, because of this, are objects of interest in themselves; but I am afraid my only reaction to their presence was one of annoyance.

It was a hot August afternoon, I had bathing-trunks with me, and I was most anxious to have a cooling dip. The sight of those dead, spear-like branches, however, deterred me. Clearly discernible from the shore while the water was undisturbed and still, it would be a different matter if a bather once started splashing about with his submarine visibility reduced to nil. The wildly superstitious tales I had heard about the fate that befell those who had the temerity to bathe in this loch did not in themselves deter me, but I had no great wish to be impaled.

I walked round to the eastern side. Here the precipitous face of Creag-nan-Gall reared up abruptly from the green water in a hill-face that was a broken jumble of jagged and multitudinous stones. I scrambled up for a dozen feet or so and looked down into the translucent depths. At this spot it was too deep for me to see the bottom, but the water was transparent enough for me to detect several very small fishes swimming about and mark its complete freedom from submerged trees. That was all I really wanted to know.

Returning to the south shore I undressed in the flower-besprinkled grass and made my way back to the steep, broken hill-face. A pause for a moment to locate submerged rocks, then a long, springing dive carried me out beyond these into the most delicious waters it has ever been my good fortune to bathe in. They were caressing, yet refreshing, and I felt I could go on swimming for hours without tiring. I trod water, I floated on my back, and then dived to a depth of three fathoms or so without gaining any glimpse of the bottom.

This, however, was a joyous experience that cannot be recommended for every visitor to this charming spot. No doubt this little hill tarn, like every other in the district, had had its sad crop of fatalities, and these, in turn, have given rise to the many discouraging tales calculated to prevent it being used as a swimming pool. Unless one is a strong swimmer and really efficient diver, I should say it is a dangerous bathing place. But, being possessed of these attributes, and being mindful to exercise due care, there is no reason why one should not enjoy the pleasure that has been mine.

There are other "Green Lochs" in the Cairngorm district, at much higher altitudes and, in every sense, true mountain tarns.

The route by the Garbhchor is the best to follow if one is to approach the Cairngorm from Revoan. Here one gets the spacious feel of the hill, even if, at the outset, there are distractions.

The first time I climbed Cairngorm I had a schoolboy nephew with me. We were making quite good time until crossing a plank-bridge over a burn. My nephew spotted two whacking great black trout, and all thought of the climb was driven out of his mind by the desire to improvise a fishing-rod without delay.

There were so many drawbacks to this plan, however, that he was at last prevailed upon to proceed, and this he did as far as the first patch of blaeberry beds. The dark, grape-coloured fruits were so large, round and inviting that I was weak enough to pause and sample; and that was the end of climbing so far as my young relative was concerned. We picked him up at Glenmore Lodge in the evening on our way home. His eyes had a glassy stare, the top button of his waistband was undone, and he had an inane grin on his face; but I doubt if I have ever seen a boy more completely pleased with himself.

Your dyed-in-the-wool mountaineering enthusiast no doubt looks down his nose at the ordinary track to the top of Cairngorm, considering it more of a long walk than a climb, but when the first flush of youth is spent such a means of getting above the 4,000 feet level is not to be sneered at, and the reward at the summit, no matter how it is achieved, is equally great for all.

A pause for a drink at the Marquis's Well, a shallow spring oozing out of the sand about 150 feet below the crest, then the next thing to do is go to the mountain's eastern edge and look down on the glory that is Loch Avon (pronounced " A'on ").[1] This hauntingly beautiful stretch of water is the gem of the Monadh Ruadh, and if you are sufficiently vigorous you may descend by one of the torrent beds, such as the Coire-domhainn, to its lovely shore.

It was near here that James Grant of Revoan found gems of a different kind; a great haul of Cairngorm stones, the largest of which, almost 50 lbs. in weight, was purchased by Queen Victoria for £50. And Cairngorms are not the only semi-precious stones that have been picked up in this locality. A little old lady of mysterious origin made an even more exciting find.

This old woman, a north-east Lowlander, was one of the many strange characters who, for one reason or another, are drawn towards residence in the Highlands. In her case, the reason was explicit. She had dreamed most vividly of finding a precious stone on the wild face of a very high mountain, and this at last brought her to the high cliff about Loch A'on.

No one in the district knew this quaint woman's name, or anything about her, other than the freely confided circumstance of her dream, so it is scarcely surprising that she was generally

[1] *See* Appendix IV.

referred to by the people of Abernethy as the *Cailleach-nan-Clach*, Old Woman of the Stone. When summer came she would disappear into the hills for weeks on end, and as her aberration was harmless, no one paid a great deal of attention to her.

Meanwhile she was painstakingly following the clues supplied in her dream, and in course of time came her reward. She found a beryl as large as a wineglass; flawless, and of rare beauty. She sold it to Mr. Winslow of Coulnakyle for a sum which, with her frugal tastes, should have kept her in comfort for the remainder of her days, but just as old prospectors are smitten with "gold fever", so was she obsessed with the desire to find more gems.

Year after year she came back to Abernethy, lodging at a conveniently situated croft and often spending several nights at a time under the Shelter Stone in Glen A'on. Once a nobleman out hunting with a party came upon her and, hearing her story, asked if she was not afraid to linger in such wild surroundings entirely alone.

"Why should I be feart?" she asked. "I ne'er see ocht waur than masel', and God is as near tae me here as he would be in Banff."

This woman found many valuable stones on the slopes of Cairngorm, though never one so perfect as her original find. Then one autumn she set off as usual to winter in the Lowlands, but when summer came she did not return. Retaining her anonymity, she simply departed from the Abernethy scene and was never heard of again.

A satisfying day on the high levels can be spent by motoring to Loch Morlich on a summer morning, and from there climbing to the top of Cairngorm before continuing along the four-mile ridge to the summit of Ben MacDuibh (4,296 feet), the second highest mountain in Britain. The return journey can be made by way of the Sron-na-Larig, with ample opportunity for pausing to look down into the awe-inspiring pass of the Larig Ghru, some 2,000 feet below.

Providing a normal pace is maintained, it is possible to spend a fair time admiring vistas that take in neighbouring peaks such as the Bynac, Cairn Toul and Braeriach, and still be home for dinner after having spent some six hours high above the world in surroundings that go to your head like wine.

That advice is intended for such as have only a limited holiday to spend in the locality, and want to take in as much of Strathspey as this will permit. For those enjoying a longer stay a leisurely hike, with nights spent in tent or bothy, is much to be preferred. In this way it is possible to linger when the prospect particularly pleases, noting all the changes in the mountain scene from the magic hour of the dawning to that breath-taking moment when the sun drops behind the western hills in all its flaming glory, bathing the hill-tops in a rosy light while pine-boughs glow a fantastic crimson and the foliage of birch trees bear a remarkable resemblance to showers of golden rain.

There is a large literature dealing with almost every aspect of the Cairngorm Mountains, so I need make no attempt here to describe each mountain in detail. One thing, though, I must not neglect; mention of the many tales concerning supernatural beings said to inhabit these regions.

Anecdotes about these are legion, and are chiefly remarkable in that they are often vouched for by witnesses of the highest integrity. There is no doubt that these persons fully believe in what they have seen or heard—phenomena apparently inexplicable by ordinary reasoning—and this particularly applies to the *Bodach Mor MacDuibh*, the "Giant Old Man of MacDuff's Mountain".

Very ancient lore names this apparition "*Am Famh*", which can mean either "giant" or "mole"; the "mole" creeping in because of the nature of certain tracks left in the snow. Here, however, he will be dealt with in his more human form.

In some accounts the Bodach Mor's actions approximate very closely to those of the Abominable Snowman, and in others (such as that supplied by John Burton of Deeside in 1864), he is described as a ferocious giant patrolling the heights above the Larig Ghru waving an uprooted pine in his hand.

This description, by the way, fits in very closely with that of Canadian Indians and backwoodsmen when it comes to describing their own pet Abominable Snowman, whom they call the "Wendigo". Among the Montaignais Indians of Northern Quebec the monster is known as the "Atchéme", and in the far North-West the Dog-rib Indians call him the "Weetinoe", but his general appearance is the same, carrying an uprooted spruce tree in one hand, and the limp body of a man in the other.

In proof of the Bodach Mor's existence in the Cairngorms we

have, first of all, the evidence of Doctor Kellas. He tells us he was on top of Ben MacDuibh one night when he saw a man climb out of the Larig Ghru and wander aimlessly in the vicinity of the cairn, passing close to where the doctor's brother was sitting. What amazed the observer was that the man appeared to be as tall as the cairn; all of ten feet high; and it also seemed strange that he should choose an hour close on midnight for a moonlight stroll alone in such surroundings.

After a time the stranger again descended into the Larig, and the doctor saw no more of him. Later, however, he asked his brother if the man had spoken to him.

" Man? " repeated his brother in surprise. " I saw no man, and I'll swear no one has been near this cairn while I've been sitting here."

That was the apparition in one form. Now, here it is in another.

In 1925, Dr. Norman Collie, a Professor of Organic Chemistry and a mountain-lover, well used to sojourning in lonely places, was returning from the cairn at the top of Ben MacDuibh when he heard the " crunch—crunch " of footsteps in his rear and, from the interval between these, knew they must be taking strides much longer than his own. He turned and peered into the mist but could see nothing. Scornfully amused that a man of his training should let his imagination play him such tricks, he continued on his way; but the eerie steps of the invisible " presence " still followed him.

What happened immediately after that he found it difficult to recall. All he was aware of was a sudden, hysterical restriction in his throat, accompanied by complete surrender to blind, unreasoning terror. Without further attempt at investigation, and utterly panic-stricken, he ran, stumbled and slid for several miles down the mountain-side, only regaining control of himself when within striking distance of Glenmore.

Surely no topic has sustained public interest over a longer period than recurring allusions to the existence of the Abominable Snowman. In Strathspey, as the Bodach Mor, he has been a subject for discussion since time immemorial, and as far back as February 8th, 1855, we find a great old stir being caused by the appearance of his tracks at Dawlish and Teignmouth, in Devon. These tracks were bi-lobal, in the shape of a large cloven hoof, and they negotiated roof-tops and high walls with a complete contempt for obstacles in any form. *The Times* featured the occurrence, the *Illustrated London News* published sketches and eye-witness accounts, while the local pulpits thundered that Satan was abroad on the business of claiming his own.

All sorts of weird theories were put forward in explanation of these tracks, laying the blame on creatures ranging from a kangaroo to some gigantic bird hitherto unknown to science, but the fact remained that not a single speculation was other than ridiculous and even less worthy of credence than the views of those who based their origin on a supernatural plane.

On December 2nd, 1952, I was reminded of the many tales I had heard relating to the Bodach Mor and other types of Abominable Snowman when, while walking about a mile from the village of Cromdale, I came across tracks every bit as mysterious as those seen in Devon almost a hundred years before. They were running across a stretch of snow-covered moorland, each print 19 inches long by about 14 inches wide, and there must have been all of 7 feet between each "stride". There was no differentiation between a right and left foot, and they proceeded in an approximately single line.

Like the Devon tracks they were bi-lobal in shape, and although there were no walls in the vicinity for them to climb, they did leap across a sunken roadway at one point for a distance of 30 feet or so. I followed the tracks for about half a mile until they terminated at the foot of a pine, for all the world as though the strange creature making them had leapt up into the foliage of the tree. Yet they did not end here, for about 20 yards farther on, in an adjoining patch of arable, I picked them up again. They traversed the little white field, plunged down the hill to the river's edge, and disappeared opposite the village churchyard.

What a perfect vanishing point for an Abominable Snowman!

The sun was dipping low towards the horizon. Like Dr. Collie, I took to my heels and ran—although not for the same reason. I wanted to collect a camera and get a picture of those tracks before the light went.

In this, I am glad to say, I was successful, and as soon as the prints were ready I showed them to several local people, including gamekeepers and ghillies. I noted the light of uneasiness in the

A RIVERSIDE CROFT. By a famous salmon pool

THE WINDING WAY. Typical secondary road in Strathspey

eyes of some as they studied the photographs, and the puzzlement in others. One ghillie stated bluntly that they were Bodach-tracks, while the rest could make no guess as to their origin.

I will confess that I should have been equally baffled but for a rather unique experience that came my way about thirty years ago.

In 1924 I was working with an exploration party in Northern Canada. One day, when snow-shoeing over a frozen lake, I came across tracks which puzzled me and reduced my companion, a French-Canadian dog-skinner, to a state of gibbering terror.

The tracks, somewhat oval in shape, looked at first glance as though they had been made by snow-shoes of the "bear-paw" type, except that they had two toe-like impressions sticking out from the main print, and ran in an almost straight single line. Their most unusual feature, however, apart from their great size, was the distance between each imprint; more than the length of a tall man. What sort of creature, I asked myself, could have been responsible for such giant strides?

My companion was only too willing to enlighten me. Crossing himself and praying in voluble French, he interspersed his supplication with remarks about the "Windygo", insisting that we get on to camp without further delay.

I examined the tracks more closely. So far as I could see they were uniform in shape and size, and the distance between them did not vary. There was, moreover, a rounding at the edges suggesting they were several days old. To me they were completely inexplicable, and I will admit I was somewhat disturbed as I gave in to my companion's pleading and continued towards camp.

Next morning our dog-skinner, together with the French-Canadian cook, had deserted down-country, and I shall always remember that first encounter with Wendigo tracks because of the inconvenience these departures caused us. But the winter survey went on, and the incident had almost faded from my mind when I again had occasion to cross the same lake—this time alone.

It was a day of brilliant sunshine with the white expanse of the snow-covered lake gleaming brightly in the frosty air. All the world was silent and still, except for the crunching of my

F

racquettes in the crisp snow. A few small scatterings of cloud suggested that a fair breeze might be blowing upstairs, although at ground level nothing of this could be felt. I was within half a mile of the shore when I saw the mysterious tracks for a second time—*on this occasion while they were actually being made!*

There, on the flawless, smooth white of the snow, a whole succession of tracks in "line-astern" were appearing miraculously before my eyes. No sign of life anywhere, no movement even, other than the drifting clouds overhead and those tracks springing suddenly into being as they came inexorably towards me.

I stood stock-still, filled with reasonless panic. The tracks were being made within 50 yards of me—20—10—then, smack! I shouted aloud as a large blob of water struck me full in the face. I swung round brushing the water from my eyes, and saw the tracks continuing across the lake.

In that moment I knew that the Wendigo, Abominable Snow-man, Bodach Mor, or what have you, was for ever explained so far as I was concerned.

Some freakish current of warm air, coming in contact with the low temperature, had set up condensation which was projected earthwards in the form of water-blobs. When these landed in the snow they left tracks like those of some fabulous animal. This time they were a little smaller than the ones I had seen on the previous occasion, nor were the prints so wide apart, but in form they were pretty much the same.

Since then, on a few rare occasions, I have encountered what I call "blob-tracks" in the Arctic and other parts of the world. I even saw them in the High Weald of Kent during the severe winter of 1939. In shape and size they have not always been uniform, varying from the bi-lobal to tracks which looked as though they might have been made by a gigantic rabbit or mole.

Water-blobs can perform every trick accredited to the Abominable Snowman. They can leave their tracks over the roofs of houses, leap high walls or cross ravines. They are, in other words, a matter for study by the meteorologist rather than the zoologist or demonologist, and are only encountered in conditions of low air temperatures.

It is an uncongenial task extracting the wonder from old beliefs and folk-tales, but the natural reason for these can also prove of interest and should not be withheld so long as the debunking is based on a sound premise.

Dr. Collie did not actually see the prints of the footsteps behind him, he only heard their "crunch", and on crisp snow falling water-blobs could have made this sound. As for Dr. Kellas and the giant he saw by the cairn, I am convinced that he was a victim of the "brocken", an optical illusion noted in the Cairngorms whereby hill mist reflects the figures of persons—sometimes greatly magnified—and makes them appear as though they belonged to someone else.

The fact that the spectre of the mountain was once described as a giant mole is capable of a two-fold explanation. Giant mole tracks could have been made by water-blobs, or the "brocken" may have magnified a stoat, or similar animal, to look like the huge creature of mythology. Stefannsson, the Arctic explorer, tells of an instance when drifting sea mist once so magnified a tiny lemming that he raised his rifle in the belief that he had come upon a musk-ox.

Of course it could be that I am quite wrong in the explanations I have put forward, and, if so, there can be no compromise on the alternative. Those tracks I found, and took the trouble to photograph, simply must have been made by the *Bodach Mor*.

CHAPTER VII

ENCHANTED WATERS

Lochs large and small – The Stirk's Loch – Black Sandy – The Kelpie of Loch Pityoulish – A different kind of monster – The lilies of Loch Garten – The Glaistig of Gartenmore – Loch of the Curse – Malediction of Mullingaroch – Loch of the Treasure – The Irishman's dream – A man who made crime pay – Springs and wells of Spey – The "boiling" spring of Rynettan – The great spring of Garbhalt – The Grants' Well – The Well of St. Maluac.

S T R A T H S P E Y has long been famed for the rich feeding qualities of its vivid green grass and the consequent sleek fatness of its black cattle; renowned everywhere from the Royal Highland Show to Smithfield, from the Argentinian pampas to the western American plains. Gregor, record-priced supreme prizewinner at the 1952 Smithfield Show, was of Strathspey stock, and so also were most of the champion black bulls that have gone to sire famous overseas herds during the past fifty years or so.

This rich quality of pasture is not to be wondered at when one notes the extent of the natural irrigation with which the great valley abounds. The streams and burns feeding the fast-flowing river must number several hundreds, and to these can be added their watersheds in the form of unbelievably lovely lochs and lochans; the last-named meaning a little loch or mountain tarn.

The smallest loch would be difficult to name, but the largest is undoubtedly Morlich, situated at an altitude of 1,045 feet, with hill and tree-bordered shores two miles long by half a mile broad. Without being exact on the point, I should say that one of the Green Lochans mentioned in an earlier chapter can claim to be the highest of these land-girt reservoirs, because one only obtains a first glimpse of it after the 3,000 feet level has been passed when climbing Cairngorm.

Apart from the mountain tarns, no two of these lochs are even approximately alike. Loch-an-Eilean, as we have already noted, is absolutely unique, and as different as it is possible to imagine from Loch Gamhna (the Stirk's Loch), separated from it by a strip of land only a few hundred yards wide.

Loch Gamhna, rather commonplace in appearance when compared with the other lochs in Strathspey, has two points worthy of notice; its summer display of water-lilies, and a nearby hole in the rocks that was once the retreat of a man known as Black Sandy.

No doubt Sandy was called "black" because of his colouring, though his deeds could have offered equal excuse for such a title. He it was who disfigured and cut off the ears of the "Bonnie housekeeper at the Croft", simply because she had borne the young laird four children out of wedlock, and his father was worried lest the estate would have to be parcelled out among a horde of illegitimate children.

This foul deed raised such an outcry against the perpetrator that he was forced to flee down the strath. Here he almost killed a man who recognized him, and then fled farther afield, this time to America.

In a previous work, unknowingly following a faulty authority, I stated that a descendant of this Black Sandy was General Ulysses Grant, who became President of the United States, but I have since learned this was not the case. General Grant was descended from one Matthew Grant, who landed in America long before Black Sandy's day, and settled at Palisado Green (now Windsor), Connecticut.

Recent inquiries on my part have brought to light the possibility that Black Sandy was, in fact, a fugitive Grant from Glenmoriston. He was noted in Rothiemurchus at a time of great political upheaval, and was probably one of the "broken men" who came into Strathspey in search of asylum. He was employed by the Laird of Rothiemurchus as a stableman, and it was doubtless a desire to curry favour with his master that caused him to commit his fearful crime.

When travelling along the eastern bank of the river from Nethybridge to Coylum Bridge one comes to a winding dip at Kincardine where the road flies over a bridge spanning a burn. From this bridge there is a really enchanting view of lovely Loch Pityoulish, whose reed-lined shore is less than a hundred yards away.

This beautiful spot is remarkably rich in associations with bygone days. Here is the hollow where the Shaws slew the Cummings, and a rocky height called Craig Chasteil (Castle Rock) still bears the ruins of a terraced fort of prehistoric times. From the roadway the Caillart can also be seen rearing up behind the eastern shore, a dip in its crest revealing the top of Cairngorm.

Apart from the appeal of its appearance, Loch Pityoulish is also notable as having once been the home of a fascinating, if fearsome, Kelpie, or Water Horse; very much akin to the White Horse of Spey and, apparently, possessed of the same endearing habits when ranging in pursuit of its prey.

The Water Kelpie of Pityoulish achieved its greatest notoriety by appearing one day to the son of the Baron of Kincardine, who was playing along the loch-shore with some companions. The youngest of these was the first to catch sight of the unearthly visitant, and there was certainly nothing horrifying in what he saw.

"Oh, look, everyone," he called out. "See the lovely pony."

All turned their heads to discover a snow-white palfrey nibbling daintily at the grass a few yards away. Saddle, bridle and stirrups of gleaming silver were encrusted with precious stones, while reins and saddle-cloth were of crimson velvet edged with gold.

The first thought of every boy present was to grab hold of such an attractive mount, and just at first it seemed as if this might be possible, because the pony allowed them to come quite close before flirting his mane and moving on a few steps—always closer to the waters of the loch.

At last one managed to seize the bridle, and the others quickly followed suit, but no sooner had they done so than, with a shrill whinny, the white pony rushed headlong for the water. It was only then that the boys discovered to their horror that instead of being captors they were captives, for when they tried to let go the reins and bridle they found their fingers were unable to release their grasp.

The Baron's son, who had managed no more than an insecure grip with two fingers of his left hand, was alone able to break loose. This he did by drawing his dirk with his free right hand and severing the fingers holding him captive. As he fell back on the green sward he saw the kelpie disappear beneath the water, dragging his six companions with it, none of them ever to be seen again.

Towards the beginning of the nineteenth century a different kind of monster dwelt in Pityoulish's peaceful-looking waters, but this was adequately disposed of by a well-known sportsman, Colonel Thornton, who later wrote at considerable length on the adventure.[1] The kelpie on this occasion was a huge pike, measuring 5 feet 4 inches long and weighing 48 lbs.

This Colonel Thornton, by the way, was very much the *de luxe* type of sportsman, and no big-game hunter going on *safari* in darkest Africa indulged in greater preparations. His assault upon the game of the strath was something in the nature of a pincer-movement, supplies flowing in to his base in Badenoch both by sea and land. A schooner deposited his extensive gear at Findhorn, and this was then taken the fifty miles overland. He shot, angled and hawked, and varied his outdoor activities by laying on sumptuous banquets under canvas to which all of the local gentry were invited. Such festivity, however, did not impair his skill in other directions. Using a single-barrelled, flint-lock gun he could bag his thirty brace of grouse in a day, and between five and eight one morning he killed five salmon; one of them weighting 42 lbs.

Another shimmering loch of considerable charm is Garten; ringed by the pine woods of Tulloch, in the parish of Abernethy. Almost three-quarters of a mile in length, by under half a mile wide, it has an air of delightful, secluded peace, and to this can be added the beauty of innumerable water-lilies, visible in the shallow water along its north-eastern shore.

Nowadays there is more than these "white cups of the morning" finding refuge in the waters of Garten. Shortly after the Second World War vast quantities of live ammunition were ferried out to its deepest area, and there allowed to sink. The general inference is that by now all this lethal material has been rendered harmless, and so far there have been no incidents to suggest the contrary.

At one time Loch Garten also had its supernatural denizen, in the form of a hoary and repellent old man, called the *Glaistig*, whose habit it was to bellow most mournfully in warning when a member of the house of Gartenmore was about to die. But

[1] *Sporting Tour in the Highlands of Scotland*, 1804, by Colonel Thornton.

there is an obvious limit to what the precursors of evil can do, and when the Gartenmore family were rendered extinct by the old fellow's delight in howling, he, perchance, found himself out of a job. In any case, he has never been heard of again since the last of the Gartenmores died.

Separated from Loch Garten by a narrow strip of thickly-wooded land lies Loch Mallachie (Loch of the Curse), the source of the Mullingarroch Burn. I have never been able to find out the nature of the curse that gave the loch its name; unless it is in some way connected with the malediction of the man who was eagerly waiting for his bride and her attendants to cross the Mullingarroch Burn. She was well, happy and smiling, and waved a greeting to her husband-to-be as she reached the stepping-stones. Then she paused uncertainly, stumbled—and dropped dead.

The bereaved lover took this blow in a most unusual manner. Instead of being content with ordinary, decorous grief he riled against the fate that had robbed him of his dear one, and called down a curse on all who might also venture to cross the burn on their wedding day.

The exact wording of this curse has not come down to us, but it must have been pretty potent because up until comparatively recent times there were still young people who preferred to make a long detour through the woods fringing Garten and Mallachie rather than cross the Mullingarroch Burn when on their way to a nuptial ceremony.

It is hardly possible, or even desirable, to enumerate all the lochs in Strathspey in a work of this scope, but before leaving the subject entirely I should like to mention just one more; not because of its impressive size or aspect (because it is really very tiny and undistinguished), but chiefly owing to the story connected with it. This is so markedly Celtic, and so typical of the tales manufactured to explain family origins that it is worthy of mention.

Loch-na-h-Ulaidh (Loch of the Treasure) is really only a lochan, and is situated in Balliefurth, on the Grantown-Nethy-bridge road. There are two versions of the legend relating to the treasure it is said to contain; but we will ignore the one about the fire guardian, who comes out of the ground as a searing flame to devour disturbers of the treasure, and concentrate on the second. This connects the treasure with a stone still standing in the wall at the east end of Balliefurth plantation.

We are told that a man in distant Ireland had a dream in which he saw treasure hidden in a place in Scotland called Strathspey. This made such an impression on him that he crossed to Scotland with all speed, landing in North Argyle and working his inquiring way eastward until he reached the parish of Abernethy. Here he saw the place marked by a stone standing on the edge of the moor, exactly as depicted in his dream.

A man named Alain-nam-foide (Alan the turf-cutter), a Cameron from Lochaber who had settled in Strathspey, was working in the nearby moss when the Irishman asked him to lend a hand in moving the stone. When they had done so, they saw a flight of steps leading down into what proved to be a treasure chamber. The Irishman loaded his spoils into a sack, made Alan a present of some trinkets and gold coin, and set off as fast as his legs could go; which amounted to no great speed owing to the weight he was carrying.

Alan, pleased with his unlooked-for riches, hurried to tell his girl-friend of his good fortune, but instead of showing the joy he expected, that young woman roundly abused him for a fool, telling him to get after the Irishman before he got clean away. She made her meaning clear.

"It's married we'll be if you can lay your hands on that gold," she told him, "and unless you do so you'll never be able to prove to me that it is only in looks you're a fool."

Thus goaded, Alan immediately set off, overtook the Irishman as he neared Castle Roy, and with one blow of his turf-cutting spade, killed him. Picking up the sack containing the treasure he returned to his sweetheart, and in due course they were married. So proud was he of his wife's practical turn of mind that he took her name, which was Grant, and his progeny were later known among the Grants as Clan Alan.

It is a pity that troublesome historians prove beyond all question of doubt that the Clan Alan are ever so much older than that particular story. But it is refreshing in these altruistic days to hear of one man so little troubled by conscience as to make crime pay.

A less spectacular, but often equally pleasing, source of water supply in Strathspey is its innumerable wells. The names of these invariably carry the prefix *fuaran* or *tobar* in accordance with their nature; the first referring to a natural spring well, and the other to one that is man-made.

On the hill-side at Carn Rynettan, near the Tulloch road, is to be found the Fuaran-ghoile (the boiling spring), but it is well to remember that this designation is only metaphorically descriptive of the spring's action, and not its temperature. Wendy Wood, in her *Secret of Spey*, tells most amusingly how she inadvertently plunged her hand into this spring and, feeling it sting, hastily withdrew it under the impression that she had been scalded. As it was a particularly wet and cold day when this happened, it is easy to appreciate her recorded disappointment when she realized it was chill, not heat, that was responsible for her reaction.

I have occasionally come upon "boiling" wells in wild spots high up in the Grampians, but these, unlike the one at Carn Rynettan, did not appear to be constant, evidently depending upon climatic conditions for their surging ebullience. I recall once looking out of the train window as we were nearing the Grampian summit and seeing a fountain gushing in a steady jet a good ten feet into the air. But this was on a day of thunderstorm and pouring rain. When next I passed that spot and looked for my "playing fountain" not the faintest trace of it was to be seen.

By far the biggest spring in Strathspey is the Fuaran-morgharbh-uilt (Great Spring of Garvalt). This is well worthy of its name, for it is at least ten feet across, the water pouring from it like a mill-race. At one time this spring-well was mistakenly supposed to be the source of the River Nethy.

Many of the wells and springs have obviously been named to commemorate persons or happenings. High up on the eastern slope of the Bynach Mor, for instance, there is the Fuaran-nan-Granndaich (Spring-well of the Grants), so called because a party of this name on a reiving expedition into Deeside once rested there.

High up in the hills near the Green Lochan is the deepest spring-well in the district, and its name, Fuaran-ghamhainn (the Stirk's spring) commemorates that such an animal once fell into it and was drowned. Considering the water in this spring is getting on for twenty feet deep, this fate of a stray beast is scarcely surprising.

The *tobars*, made by men who liked the fruits of their labours to be duly sanctified, generally show in their names some connection with church or saint. Tobar-Fettle on the Grantown Bridge of Brown road, and Tobar-Thomhaldidh in Kincardine, are both named after old Celtic saints, while in Abernethy there is Tobar-Donaich, the Lord's Day Well.

A notable well in Cromdale is situated on the river bank near the girder bridge. Because of its connection with a tenth-century Celtic saint this is known as St. Maluac's Well. The present residents at the Boat House draw their water from here, and in all history it has never been known to fail; which is another way of saying it has been in constant use for over a thousand years.

That engenders quite a thought. Many changes are wrought in local natural features through the years—in my own time I have known a burn to change its course on many occasions, and there are now productive fields where lochs stood less than a hundred years ago—yet if the sainted Maluac returned to this neighbourhood to-morrow he would still find one feature completely unchanged; his old drinking well.

CHAPTER VIII

A GLANCE AT THE "GOOD" OLD DAYS

Courts of Regality – The Baillie Barons – Drowning Pools and Hanging Hills – The Baillie Mor – The Baillie Roy – The murder of the Baillie Bain – Quip by a Cromdale man – Brigadier Grant as judge – Crimes and Punishments – The scourging of Fair Margaret – Problems of maintaining the law – Kirk Session Records – Unholy documents – The case of the schoolmaster – Dr. Forsyth's view of old Church discipline – The Famine of King William – Years of dread – A horrible pestilence – The "treasure" of Tullochgorm – The Hen Wife – The year of the Short Crop – The great flood of '29 – Sir Thomas Dick Lauder's description of same.

No book dealing with this part of the world, published within the last hundred years, has failed to mention the Regality Courts, or the notorious rule of the Baron Baillies. There are five Court Books of the Regality of Grant still in existence. These record Court business covering the period 1690-1729, and in this day of vociferous social consciousness they make the grimmest of grim reading.

These Courts were the instrument of heritable jurisprudence, whereby the Lord of the Manor had rights of pit and gallows over his tenantry, and although it was in the actual Laird of Grant that this power rested for most of the parishes in Strathspey, the practice of many Grant Chiefs was to delegate the duty to a representative who was known as the Baillie Baron.

To thus elevate a man to a position where he held the lives and possessions of his neighbours in the hollow of his hand was, perhaps, to ask too much of human nature. The Baillie was entitled to confiscate the goods of the prisoner he had tried and condemned to death, as well as being permitted to retain all fines imposed by him in the course of his duty. One Baillie made such a good thing out of his term of office that he was able to lend the Laird the sum of 22,000 merks, and ultimately retired with a fortune of about £4,000; a very considerable sum in those days.

Not all the Baillies abused their trust, and there were even

Lairds of Grant who shouldered their responsibilities to the extent of performing the onerous task of Regality judge themselves but all the evidence goes to prove that these were much in the minority.

Ballintomb, near the junction of the Dulnain with the Spey, was the chief centre where the court was held, but there were also sittings in other places, when the convenience of witnesses had to be considered.

Various sites were used throughout the Strath for implementing the court's findings, each in accordance with the nature of the sentence. Witches and other women criminals were executed in the Drowning Pool at Balliemore, while male prisoners were dispatched on Gallows Trees up and down the river. Perhaps the most famous of these improvised gibbets was that at Lynestock, sometimes called the "Tree of the Brothers"; innocent victims of Robert Grant, known as the "Baillie Mor". Other *Tom-a-chrochair*, or Hangman's Hills, are to be found at Rothiemoon and Cromdale. The actual tree no longer stands at the latter place, but it was situated on the hill adjoining my former dwelling, close to the ruins of Croft-na-Malloch (the Cursed Croft).

The Baillie Mor was a complete brute and bully who took full advantage of the omnipotent power granted him by careless circumstance. He invariably held court without a jury and, as in the case of the two brothers, was known to hang people for no other reason than that they had disobliged him.

Even worse than the Baillie Mor was James Grant, called the "Baillie Roy", or Red Baillie. One of his victims, a man named Steuart, industrious, God-fearing and hard-working, had committed no crime other than to arouse the Baillie Roy's covetousness at the quality and extent of his cattle and possessions. Poor Steuart was seized and dragged before the Baillie on a trumped-up charge. On this occasion the Baillie Roy used a jury to find the prisoner guilty; but only *after* he had already been hanged. No sooner was the sentence carried out then Steuart's goodly possessions were seized, and his wife and children turned out to go begging. The shock was too much for the poor woman. She became mentally deranged and a few weeks after her husband's death her body was fished out of the Nethy.

But the worst of all the Baron Baillies was the "Baillie Bain", or Fair Baillie. His deeds are too harrowing to recount, but their enormity can be gauged by the fact that his down-trodden victims were driven to open revolt. One day when he was riding along the banks of the Spey near the church of Inverallan, a hostile crowd swooped down upon him and let him feel the bite of cold steel. His assailants took off his boots and gloves and left them on the bank to inform searchers that the man they were seeking was in the river, then they quietly dispersed.

Next day a party out looking for the body came upon a man near the church of Cromdale, a little more than four miles down-stream from where the Baillie Bain was presumed to have been thrown into the water. They told this man what they were searching for, and asked if he had seen anything.

" I have not, and I'm sure neither will you," was his reply.

" Why are you so certain? " asked a searcher.

" Because the Baillie Bain was ever one to go against nature," said the Cromdale man, " so it's *upstream* you should be searching, not down."

This Baillie Bain was the last of the Baillie Barons. The fate meted out to him drew the attention of the Laird of Grant, in this case Brigadier Alexander Grant, to the sorry state to which the Regality Court had fallen, and he himself took over the administration of justice from then on.

One of the first things he learned was that many thieves and law-breakers had been plying their lawless trade with impunity simply because they had bought the protection of the Baillie Bain. On assuming office the Laird rounded up eight of his clansmen known to be so shielded, and promptly hanged the lot of them.

Judged by present standards, some of Brigadier Grant's sentences seem little less reprehensible than those of his fore-runners, but before being condemnatory it is well to remember the conditions of that particular period.

Reiving and freebooting in those days was not so much a question of ethics as of economic necessity. Farming methods were based on a mixture of superstition and sheer incompetence. and the food grown, even when subsidized by the slaughter of deer and other game, was not nearly sufficient to sustain the population in some of the over-settled glens. A man very often had to raid or thieve to live, and when arrested there were no prisons where he could be punished or put out of harm's way.

He knew that if he were caught committing certain crimes his life was forfeit, and, as the rules of the game were clearly understood, he never questioned the justice of this. His job was to break the law without being captured or found out. If he failed in this, then he had no kick coming.

The following brief selections from the Court Books of the Regality of Grant offer a fair example of the crimes and punishments of those turbulent days. The extracts are paraphrased into modern English:

Resetting of stolen wool: The wife of William MacAndrachie Mor, in Lynegarrow, fined £20 Sc. for resetting wool stolen by her daughter from Duncan Roy, in Gartenmore.

Scourged at the Gallows Tree for theft: 13th, November, 1696. Patrick Bain of Reinacleaunch and his daughter are convicted of theft. His friends become security for his good conduct for three years, and to see that he is produced in Court at the end thereof. Baillie Grant ordains that he shall be taken immediately to the Gallows Tree at Ballintomb, tied thereto by the executioner with a hempen cord, his body made naked from the waist upward, and then to suffer twenty-four stripes from the executioner to the effusion of his blood. After this he will be let go. . . . His daughter, Margaret, will also be tied by the executioner to the Gallows Tree and her body made naked from the waist upward. She will receive thirty stripes, until the blood be made to run down, and after this she will be banished from Strathspey, never to return under pain of death.

Scourged at Regality Cross, Grantown, 1703: For haunting with the notorious freebooter called the Halkit Stirk, and other outlaws, Margaret Bain, now residing at Inchtomach, to be taken to the Regality Cross at Grantown, tied thereto, stripped from the waist upward, and given thirty stripes by the executioner until the blood be made to run down. After this she will have one ear cut off, and be banished from Strathspey, never to return under pain of death.

Strange case of drunkenness: Three women charged with smuggling whisky to prisoners in ward at Castle Grant, whereof several drank to such excess that they died, to be taken to the Regality Cross at Grantown, stripped from the waist upward and tied thereto by the executioner, and each receive thirty stripes.[1]

[1] These women were scourged on the same day as Margaret Bain.

Breach of Sabbath, 20th November, 1706: John Stewart Roy of Congash fined £20 for bargaining upon the Sabbath Day.

Burning heather: Alexander Gardiner, alias Murray, Patrick John Dhu, miller, Patrick Barron, son of David Barron, convicted of burning heather adjacent to the rear of Craigmore, Abernethy, whereby much fir wood was burned. To be taken to the gallows on the moor of Ballintomb, and to have their lugs nailed to same.

Theft of cheese: John Barron, son of David Barron, Abernethy, broke into the house of John Fraser, stole his cheese, and committed other thefts. An assize sat upon him, and found him, together with William MacAndachie, to be guilty of the charges preferred against them. They have been adjudged common thieves, who have been trading in theft for a very long time, and can find no surety. Both to be hanged on 20th August, on the Hanging Hill at Ballintomb.

Breach of trust: James Grant of Rymore, late forester of the woods of Abernethy, is fined £100 Sc. for not handing over to the Laird of Grant money received from sale of wood to the people.

At first glance some of these sentences may appear unduly savage; yet when we examine them more closely we learn something of the problems with which the law was then faced.

The name Margaret Bain, or Fair Margaret, is apt to conjure up a picture of a beautiful girl falling a victim to sheer brutality, but then let us consider that her name was purely descriptive of her colouring (in that she was the opposite from dark) and note that she is convicted of theft and habitually consorting with thieves. On one occasion, after scourging, she is banished under pain of death, but when she ignores the court's ruling and is again captured the death sentence is not carried out. Under such circumstances, a further scourging and the loss of an ear probably appeared to the populace of the time as particularly lenient treatment.

It should also be noted that John Barron was not hanged merely for stealing a cheese. He was a habitual criminal, no doubt convicted on many previous occasions, and, with no penal settlement to commit him to, there was only one rational means of putting an end to his activities.

The salutary lesson of having an ear nailed to a tree may seem

BALLINDALLOCH. Where main highway crosses bridge at castle entrance

THE CASTLE STRIPE. With highway bridge over the Avon at Ballindalloch

very barbarous in these enlightened days, but irresponsible fire-raisers who destroy valuable property are a menace to any community, and their callous, anti-social behaviour could just as easily have been responsible for loss of life. Patrick Barron, one of the men who had his ear nailed, is brother to John Barron, condemned to be hanged as an inveterate law-breaker and thief. This suggests that the three prisoners were a thoroughly bad lot and, as such, in need of a very sharp lesson.

By and large, providing one can omit the excesses of the Baillie Barons already named, the law-abiding citizens of those days probably had little more to fear from the secular authority than they have to-day. But they had another arbiter of conduct ruling their lives that often proved well-nigh intolerable; the inquisitorial dictatorship of the Kirk Session.

How a proud and independent people could have submitted to such gross interference with their personal actions and liberty would be beyond understanding if one did not remember that the Kirk Session had the backing of the Regality Court. This meant that any parishioner refusing submission to the church discipline could be passed on to the secular court, and there summarily dealt with.

There are many manuscript volumes of Kirk Session Records still in existence. Sometimes they are to be found in local manses; at others in Record Offices, such as the Tolbooth in Edinburgh. Without exception, they can be detected immediately by their odour—not of sanctity but the charnel house—and their written content is as nauseating as the foulness of their smell.

It is true that they contain *some* matters of interest, such as the records dealing with the "Management of the Poor", but a good 97 per cent of the items mentioned come under the heading of "Discipline", and it is these that are so lamentable.

I was looking through a volume of Session Records only a short time ago. It had about thirty-three lines of entries to each page dealing with discipline, and according to these a Christian could, apparently, commit only the sin popularized in the Garden of Eden. It was noted with monotonous repetition, the entries generally followed by orders for the recalcitrants to stand on the "Stool of Repentance" before the whole congregation on a requisite number of Sundays. In a cash column to the right of each page the fines exacted were duly set down. In the particular records I am referring to, these mostly ranged from 15s. to 16s. 8d.; although the virtue of one young woman was priced as high as £2 6s. 8d., without reason for this being given.

One of their most revolting entries, however, was the frequently recurring "Delation for ante-nuptial fornication". Under this heading I came across one case which reveals how pernicious this procedure of church discipline could be. This is what happened:

A young schoolmaster came to a certain parish in Strathspey and took over the duties of Session Clerk; an office schoolmasters have been called upon to fill in rural Scotland for a long time. The new clerk married a very respectable young woman, and about seven months afterwards his wife gave premature birth to a child; the clerk, evidently knowing his Session and not taking any chances, obtained a certificate from the doctor to this effect.

At first only congratulations came the way of the happy young parents, but some months later, when attending a Session meeting, the schoolmaster was dumbfounded to learn that he had been suspended from the clerkship and arraigned to answer a charge of ante-nuptial fornication.

The schoolmaster's chief accuser was an elder whose wife, as the local howdy, had helped at the birth of the child. This good Christian asserted that she knew too much about midwifery not to recognize a nine months' birth when she saw it, and that this child was not at all premature. In this she was evidently far ahead of the doctor who signed the certificate, for, when further questioned, all he could say was that he fully believed the birth to be premature, without being able definitely to prove it.

In desperation the poor schoolmaster sought the help of another doctor (whose wife, a nonagenarian who died only a few years ago, was well known to me), but the latter had not seen the baby until it was two weeks old and could not, therefore, offer a positive opinion. He did state, however, that although he could not prove the birth was premature, neither could anyone else establish it otherwise.

That, then, was the evidence the Kirk Session had to consider; one doctor who expressed full belief that the birth was premature, and another who, without committing himself, implied that it might well be. Against this qualified opinion there was only the uncharitable conclusions of a peasant woman.

The Session duly deliberated—and found in favour of the mid-wife's reckoning.   The schoolmaster was delated and, without right of appeal, dismissed from his clerkship and school.

The Rev. Dr. Forsyth has much to say about the Kirk Sessions in his book *In the Shadow of Cairngorm*.   In one chapter he remarks:

"It has been said that the evil men do lives after them.   This holds true, though in a different sense from what Shakespeare meant, as to Session Records.   While there is much that is good in these old books, the evil certainly predominates. . . . Two things strike one forcibly in reading these records—first, the vast-ness of the claims of the Church in supervising the conduct of the people, and then the ineffectiveness of the methods pursued for this purpose.   In the present day the complaint is often made that the Church has lost power, and that discipline is not carried out.   This may be true; but whatever may be done in the way of reform, there will be no disposition to go back to the rude and repulsive ways of our fathers.   The cutty stool is gone for ever. In our parish (Abernethy) the last instance of public rebuke was in the days of Mr. Martin.   The usual notice had been given. Then the ladies of the congregation concerted what they would do.   When Mr. Martin called upon the culprits to come forward, Mrs. Grant, Birchfield, and Mrs. MacDonald, Coulnakyle, from the galleries, and Mrs. Gordon, Revack, and Mrs. Forsyth, Dell, from the body of the church, rose and walked out.   This silent protest had the desired effect."

Uncomfortable though life must have been under two such incubi as Regality Courts and Kirk Sessions, man-made evils were not the only trials resident in Strathspey had to contend with in the long ago.   There were, for instance, climatic vagaries, natural upheavals such as earthquake and flood, and the terrible *Gort Righ Uilleam*, or Famine of King William.

This last occurred towards the close of the seventeenth century, when King James the Seventh had fled over the water and William of Orange sat on his throne.   There was nothing in the spring of that year to suggest that it might differ greatly from others, yet by the time high summer was scheduled a biting east wind was sweeping the strath, followed by a yellow fog that blanketed the haughs and hid the high tops of the bens.

Each day as the sun reached its zenith this fog dispersed, but by late afternoon it had formed again. This continued day after day and night after night until, with the chill soaking through the hours of darkness and the fierce scorching of the noonday sun, the half-filled corn was struck with a strange form of mildew.

Instead of yellowing, the grain shrivelled to a ghastly, bleached white, giving fields a snow-covered appearance, while the green tops of the root crops went to the opposite extreme and blackened as though devastated by fire.

At this time communications and international trading were not what they are to-day, and the effects of failure of a crop on which everyone depended for food can be readily imagined; yet, though disastrous, this was but a beginning. Worse—much worse—was to follow.

For seven consecutive years (1694-1701) the climate was such that summer was almost indistinguishable from winter; cold winds, rain, sleet and snow being the daily portion through all the seasons, while the fleeting appearances of the sun were but a taunt rather than harbingers of hope or joy. The grass never lost its winter tinge, the cattle were mere bony frames, birds died by the hundreds of thousands, and scarcely a fly or insect was to be seen after the month of July had gone.

Never before were dwellers in our countryside forced to face such soul-destroying conditions, yet the husbandman on farm and croft still strove to grow food, the children being sent out into the fields at what should have been harvest-time to pick the few sound grains from blasted ears of corn in an effort to ensure seed for the next year's sowing.

Such harvesting as was carried out during these abnormal years took place in January or February, the corn often having to be cut among ice and snow. It is, therefore, scarcely surprising that the ill-nourished people who were forced to labour under such conditions at last began to fall sick of a mysterious disease, the initial symptoms of which were practically unnoticeable, but whose outcome was invariably death of a particularly horrible kind. As one old local historian put it:

"Strange fevers and infectious running sores that even the oldest and most skilled physicians knew not how to treat, spread throughout the land, but though we in the Highlands were sorely

affected it was really in the low-lying parts of the country that
the dire effects of the pestilence were felt to the full."

So virulent was the disease, and so swift its progress, that people
who were in apparent good health in the evening were found
dead in their dwellings on the following morning, "*the head
resting on the hand and arms and the face not infrequently
gnawed by rats, of which there were numbers such as had never
before been known*".

Needless to say, with such fell scourges ravishing the strath,
the anecdotes left to be handed down from father to son were
many and varied. From these we can get a pretty clear picture
of what famine and pestilence in a remote and self-supporting
area can mean.

When famine alone had to be contended with, instances of
selflessness were few and rare. Every man's problem was then
a purely personal one—the eternal search for something to eat,
and the need to ease the craving in his belly. People could think
of nothing but food, and a total disregard of all else rendered
impotent the word of the Gospel or the teachings of religion in
any shape or form. They no longer acted like human beings,
and frankly admitted that they cared not whether they went to
heaven or hell so long as their pangs of hunger were allayed.

Many of the poorer families, too proud to beg and too honest
to steal, sat in their homes staring at the floor until their eyes
glazed over and sight failed them. Members of the respectable
tacksman class paid inflated prices for food, watching their life's
savings dwindling to nothing as they did so, and at last reached
a stage where they also had no idea where their next meal was
coming from. Only the very wealthy appeared properly
equipped to weather such a storm.

With the coming of the pestilence the whole picture changed.
This was no respecter of persons, and the entire population,
regardless of rank and position, was exposed to its ravaging
power. Then it was, with horrible death stalking silently among
all and sundry, that the teaching of the Gospel again came into
its own.

In one Strathspey village the laird's wife was seen helping a
newly-made widow to convey to the kirkyard the dead body of
her husband; strapped to a hand-made sled. When they reached
the cemetery another woman said to them: "You must come

with me now and help me to bring out the bodies of my daughter and two sons."

For many months the grim plague raged, not a nook or cranny being spared its visitation. Survivors from low-country towns came up into Strathspey in search of refuge among the woods and hills, but the scourge tracked them to their hiding-places and they succumbed under the open sky.

In every parish of Strathspey it is possible to come across the ruins of what once were clachans. Sometimes sheer economic pressure is the explanation why these have been allowed to sink into desuetude, but certain it is that some are grim reminders of the time of pestilence when whole rows of houses in clachan and town were burned to the ground in an effort to keep the plague from spreading.

In the same way little cairns are occasionally encountered where places of burial were chosen either for their convenience or the easy workability of the soil. On a sandy knoll near Tullochgorm a grave was hurriedly scooped out for a shepherd who had died close by, and, by one of those queer confusions traditions undergo at times, this came, within a space of fifty years, to be linked with a tale of treasure buried by some Jacobites after " the '45 ".

A new-comer to the Tullochgorm district, a ghillie, hearing this buried treasure story, determined to test the truth of it some night when the moon was bright enough to show him what he was doing. At last such a night arrived, and taking along a shovel he made short work of the grave's covering of sand. But all he found for his pains was some human bones and a few tattered fragments of Grant tartan.

Next morning he told an acquaintance of what he had done, at the same time speaking scoffingly of the treasure story. By the afternoon he was seized with a strange fever that caused his flesh to break out in offensive sores. A few days later he was dead.

One effect of the famine years was greatly to reduce the income of certain lairds, even though the rents of their tenants were more often paid " in kind " than in hard cash. At Castle Grant the person responsible for collecting these rents " in kind " was Maggie Sinclair, and her position in the household was considered of sufficient importance for her to have her portrait painted by the artist, Waitt, during the months he spent at the castle as the employed guest of the Laird.

At one time Maggie had received as rent commodities such as meal from the miller, or milk, honey and cattle from the farmer, but in the years following the famine this variety was contracted to cover no more than capons and eggs, with the result that the castle's rent collector soon became generally known by the soubriquet "Hen Wife".

Her portrait is still at Castle Grant, but is no longer hung. Like many interesting paintings by Waitt and other artists it is stacked in the corner of an empty room, where it has already suffered considerable damage.

Waitt's fees were ridiculously low—at Inverdruie House, Rothiemurchus, a detailed account for the painting of the Spreckled Laird, including materials, amounts to only a few shillings—and this undoubtedly prompted the uninformed to sneer at his artistic talent. Descendants of some of his subjects, however, are in themselves living proofs of his skill as a portraitist, their features showing beyond question his ability to paint a telling likeness.

This artist's works are to be found in other notable Highland dwellings, such as Beaufort Castle, home of Lord Lovat, and the suggestion is here made that some appropriate body contrive an exhibition of his works. Their quality is much higher than many people imagine.

Another suggestion is that Waitt's excellent portrait of the Rev. James Chapman, at present stacked with the Hen Wife on the floor of an empty castle room, should be removed to the wall of the vestry in Cromdale Kirk, where he worked and lived so happily for so long.

But to return to climatic phenomena. Since those seven terrible years of dread, Strathspey has had other uncomfortable visitations. 1826 was known as the *Bliadhna-bharr-ghoirid*, the Year of the Short Crop, and, such are the living links with the past, I know a man, now in his seventies, who was brought up by an aunt who was born in that year. She was a very old woman when she died, and when asked her age she invariably replied: "I was born three years before the flood."

The flood she referred to was, of course, the great Moray Flood of 1829, the first sign of which was a strange black cloud seen

mounting over the Moray Firth on the particularly sultry evening of Saturday, 1st of August. Gradually it took the shape of a
huge spiral column swirling up between sea and sky, growing
blacker and more terrifying as the night advanced. Then it
began to move slowly inland; only breaking when it came in contact with the peaks of the Monadhliaths west of Kingussie. This
was early on Sunday morning. In a matter of minutes torrents
of water were rushing down every channel, and each tiny stream
was swollen far beyond its normal size.

Sir Thomas Dick Lauder, whose home at Relugas was in grave
danger of destruction by the swollen waters of the Findhorn
rising fifty feet above their usual level, is recognized as the
historian of this disaster. This is how he pictures the scene:

"The noise was a distinct combination of two kinds of sound—
one a uniformly continued roar, the other like rapidly repeated
discharges of many cannons at once. The first of these proceeded
from the violence of the waters; the other, which was heard
through it, came from the enormous stones which the stream
was hurling over its bed of rock. Above all this was heard the
fiend-like shriek of the wind, yelling as if the demon of desolation
had been riding upon its blast. . . . There was something heart-
sickening in the aspect of the atmosphere. The rain was
descending in sheets, not in drops, and there was a peculiar and
indescribable lurid, or rather bronze-like, hue that pervaded the
whole face of nature as if poison had been abroad in the air."

The River Spey and its tributaries above Kingussie were
practically unaffected, but below this point it was a very different story, and by the time the main stream reached Ballindalloch
its raging waters had swamped the whole of the rich pastures in
the broad valley. The devastation and destruction of property
was appalling, but, fortunately, there was very little loss of life.

In recent years, the vagaries of weather that come readiest to
mind are, first, the sixteen degrees of frost which unexpectedly
descended upon us on the 8th of August, a number of years ago,
and the terribly cold winter of 1946-47, when there were only
three days between the 15th of December and the 9th of April
that the thermometer did not drop below freezing point. During this winter the frost went five feet into the ground, and the
whole water supply system of the village of Carrbridge was completely ruined. This resulted in the popular Carrbridge Hotel

remaining closed throughout 1947, having to cancel all summer bookings, and suffering considerable financial loss as a result.

I once heard a summer visitor to Strathspey comment that the local people seemed to be unduly preoccupied with the weather. And why shouldn't they be? They live in a northern mountain country, and weather in such regions, especially in winter, when temperatures can drop far below zero, can have a dramatic quality unknown to those who live in more sheltered surroundings.

CHAPTER IX

ON THE WESTERN BANK

*Glen of the Heroes – Mausoleum of the Grants – Gibbon Mor –
Cummings of the Hen-stone – Bigla Cumming – Her salmon-trap –
The Bonnet Stone of Kinveachy – The cauldron at the Saint's Well
– The Curse of Clury – Clury to-day – Muckrach Castle – Dulnain
Bridge – Grantown-on-Spey – An example of town-planning – A novel
advertisement – Grantown to-day.*

O F all the places in Strathspey giving a home to cairns, the
parish of Duthil, on the western bank of the river opposite Kincardine and Abernethy, must be able to stake a claim as one of
the largest burial grounds in the north. If the ancient custom
is any criterion—whereby every man, before going into battle,
placed his stone on a cairn and then collected it if he survived—
then the number of warriors who left their stone " for the count "
here must outshine in casualties even the great battles of World
War I.

These multitudinous stone memorials are explained in the old
Gaelic name for Duthil, *Gleinn-a-Chearnaich*, or Glen of the
Heroes, and the Chiefs of Grant helped to carry on this tradition
by using the churchyard at Duthil as their family burial place.
The mausoleum of granite, containing the remains of the chiefly
house since 1585, was last opened to receive the coffin of the
greatly respected Caroline, Countess of Seafield, and as that lady
left a directive in her will that the vault be permanently closed
after her admission, future Chiefs of the Clan will have to decide
upon a new resting place.

Most of the best-known traditions of Duthil parish concern
the Cumming family, who were in possession here before the
Grants arrived, although the earliest recorded owners were the
Celtic Earls of Strathearn. Many of the most popular tales are
applied to Gibbon Mor Cumming and his daughter, Bigla, but
how much credence can be placed in any of them it would be
difficult to say.

Sir William Fraser questions whether this Bigla, or Matilda,

"This is Ian Dhu Gear I have talking to me, and surely you've been told that no deer is safe while he is around."

"Would you be trying to make out that I don't know the difference between a deer and a horse?" asked Ian Dhu Gear quietly.

"That's what I've heard tell," laughed Colin as he turned to walk away.

But he didn't go far. Two strides and he was lying on the sward, with Ian wiping the blood from his *sgian* on his kilt.

"This time no one will interfere with my cache," said Ian grimly, after he had buried his victim too deep down into the ground for anyone to find. Then, as a final gesture, he set the dead Colin's bonnet on top of a tall stone as an intimation to searchers that the man they were looking for would never be seen again.

Ever since, the tall standing stone at Kinveachy has been called the "Bonnet Stone".

A tale of another kind tells how Alan Mor, Laird of Clury, came to Duthil one day and was treated to a strange vision. Visiting the Saint's Well, he was about to take a drink of water when he smelt burning, and turned to see a blazing fire roaring under a large cauldron, only a few yards away. Approaching closer he was amazed to see that the cauldron was filled with what he took at first to be a host of tiny snow buntings, but which on closer inspection proved to be the fluttering souls of unshriven children. He was then aware that the roaring of the fire was forming words, and these were being repeated in a song.

> "Cleanse, cleanse, boil and cleanse;
> Only souls baptized and shriven,
> Can ever hope to enter heaven."

The Laird was filled with a great pity for the souls of the infant innocents, and begged the fire that he should be allowed to take the cauldron back to Clury with him. Twice he made this request without response, but on his asking for a third time the fire replied that the cauldron would be his if he was prepared to accept the curse that went with it. After some hesitation, the man of Clury said he was willing to accept even that.

"Then take it," said the fire, "and there will not stand in the gathering of Strathspey but one bonnet for three generations of those who may come after you."

This rather involved pronouncement really meant that no sons would grace the house of Clury for three generations, and it is said that the curse was duly carried out. After that Clury was for long considered an unlucky place to live, but any old spells it may have carried have long since been broken.

The present Laird of Clury, Mr. James Waddell, has wrought many improvements in the old place and has enjoyed considerable success as a breeder of black cattle. Both bonnet and airaisaidh have stood under his roof. But of the cauldron there is no longer any sign. The belief is that it returned whence it came, and that the "Curse of the Man of Clury" went with it.

Not far from Duthil stand the ruins of Muckrach Castle, home of the Clan Patrick Grants until they moved to tighten their grip on their new possessions in Rothiemurchus. At one time this castle had a watch-tower, courtyard, vaulted basements and extensive outbuildings, but now only crumbling outer walls and a portion of the watch-tower remain. This last has the remnants of a spiral staircase that once served the upper floors, but now, like Jacob's ladder, has no destination other than heaven.

The road from here to Dulnain Bridge, for the greater part of the distance, keeps close to the delightful River Dulnain, a wild-looking, boulder-strewn stream banked by a variety of tall trees whose foliage often meets overhead, giving the turbulent waters the appearance of rushing through a tunnel.

The road turning to the right over the bridge, in the centre of the village, leads back up the strath and also to the appropriately named Broomhill, while the one continuing straight ahead leads to Grantown. Here the river, which for so long has been dropping down to the north, takes a sharp swing to the east, leaving Inverness-shire and entering Moray at the New Spey Bridge. It maintains this direction until the lower Craigellachie is reached, a further twenty-two miles downstream, and then resumes its former northern course to the sea.

Unlike some larger towns, Grantown-on-Spey, to give it its full name, needs no descriptive sub-title to lend it individuality. Perth, for instance, is dubbed "The Gateway to the Highlands", and Inverness "The Capital of the Highlands", yet these labels do nothing to differentiate their appearance from hundreds of other undistinguished towns in the Scottish Lowlands. In Grantown-on-Spey, however, the geographical location is never in doubt, for it is one of the most perfect examples of a little Highland town to be met with north of the Grampians.

It is debatable whether *Am-Bhaiale-Ur,* or the New Town, as the Gaelic speaking locals first called Grantown, would ever have come into being if a party of Grants had not been driven from Cromdale by clan rivals after a quarrel and sought shelter by the castle gates; but there is certainly nothing accidental in how the town assumed the appearance that we know to-day.

If ever there was an example of successful town-planning, this is it, and in conception and execution the responsibility for this must rest with two men, Sir Ludovick and Sir James, both Lairds of Grant. They had no beneficent State to aid them in their project; and in this *could* have lain some reason for their success. Theirs was no pipe-dream conceived by a Civil Servant in distant Whitehall, but the practical planning of men who knew the requirements of local conditions and had the advantage of living right on the spot.

One of the first things Sir Ludovick realized was that to make his project successful he must find people used to town life, and as the people of Strathspey were more expert in gralloching a deer than in the manufacture of marketable goods, he decided that the best way to find a population for the new town was by advertisement. He inserted a notice in an Aberdeen journal in 1766, following it up by a further advertisement in 1768. A glance at the second gives some idea of the publicist's technique in a former day.

"Ther's nine annual mercats of Fairs holds at Grantown, for Cattle, Horses, Sheep, Tissiker, Woll, etc, and Weekly Mercats. It's centrical for the South Country, Badenoch or Strathearn Dealers, or Drovers in the Low Country, as it is not above 18 miles either from Inverness, Fort George, Nairn, Forres, Elgin, Keith, or Strathboggie, and good patent roads to each of them. The Mercats are, and will be for some time, customs free. There is established a good schoole for teaching Latin, English, writing, Arithmetick, and Book-keeping, and two Weemen Schools for Sewing and Knitting of Stocking, and a fine new church to be built within the town."

I am afraid that, even when making allowance for the old Scots mile, the worthy town-planner allowed his advertising zeal to run away with him when it came to estimating distances, for both Inverness and Elgin are more than thirty miles from Grantown, with Keith and Strathbogie farther still.

If Sir Ludovick was the original architect of Grantown, his son, the "Good Sir James", was the one mainly responsible for turning early plans into reality.

He made roads, built bridges, and erected a Town House and Jail out of his own privy purse, spending more than £5,000. He also visualized a school for children where not only ordinary education but specialized instruction in trades and the Arts might be given; in this way anticipating the technical education of our own day.

Twenty years after its inception we find Grantown with a population of close on 400, representative of many trades and callings. These included tailors, shoemakers, bakers, weavers, blacksmiths, carpenters, masons, and twelve merchants who kept regular shops.

With regard to the shops, it is interesting to note that one of the original feus, Lot 17, was granted to "John Burgess, taylor," and there is still a tailor named Burgess in Grantown's High Street to-day. These Burgesses have a long connection with Strathspey, their name being mentioned in a document dealing with Abernethy as far back as 1602. This was at a time when, as Tytler says, strife in the Highlands "spread like the moor-burning of their savage districts", and Alan Burgess in Abernethy is noted answering the Grant Chief's call to arms.

Grantown to-day, with a population of something over 1,500, is the centre of a prosperous agricultural area which specializes in catering for the tourist and holiday trade. It has many excellent hotels, three of them being fully licensed, and for visitors there are special "seasonal" membership rates for the Tennis and Golf Clubs and the Strathspey Angling Association. But probably its greatest amenity is its central situation in the strath, almost equidistant, as it is, from the upper and lower Craigellachies. Local shopping facilities range from adequate to very good, and the shopkeepers are a friendly lot who have the happy knack of making a visitor feel very much at home.

Nowhere else in Britain is it possible to find a town of compar-

THE RIVERSIDE IN WINTER   Cromdale Church and Manse in sub-zero weather

THE OPEN
STRATH IN
WINTER

The author's
home at
Ballintian,
Cromdale

able size so blessed with attractive walks within a four miles radius of its centre. These go by woodland path, along the banks of river and burn to hill-tops with a commanding view; or over wild, heather-clad moorland, and have the added charm that each and all are entirely unspoiled by the hand of man.

Yes, those two old Lairds of Grant planned well, and it is not only their own people who have benefited from their industry and vision. I know one city man who has not missed an annual vacation in Grantown since before World War I.

H

CHAPTER X

TALES OF BLACK MAGIC

Three types of folk-tales – Black Magic in recent times – Variations on a theme – The Dowager of Delfruin – The wicked Captain MacPherson – The Hellish Man – The Lady of Castle Clash.

THE folk-tales of the Celt might be divided under three headings; the purely heroic, of which the Norse influence may have been the inspiration; the fanciful fairy-tale, carrying the unmistakable hall-mark of the Milesian Celt; and the weird and terrifying, perhaps introduced to Gaeldom by one of the early conquering races, such as the *Tuatha de Danaan*, possessors of the *Liath Fail*, or Stone of Destiny, and experts in the black arts of necromancy.

Whatever the explanation so far as the last-mentioned variety is concerned, the fact remains that in the truly Celtic parts of these islands, such as Eire and the Scottish Highlands, an interest has long been revealed in demonolatry, with weird beliefs concerning the subject still surviving at the present day.

In 1942 a case was reported in the national press to the effect that the inhabitants in a certain area of the North-west Highlands were forced to call in the police to take action against a local laird, notorious in the neighbourhood as a dabbler in the Black Arts. According to the complainants, uncouth, unearthly shapes were haunting the fields and lonely roadways after dark and the populace became so terrified that they refused to quit their homes after nightfall, even in parties of two or three.

Had it not been that the Second World War was then at its height the series of phenomena described would undoubtedly have supplied front-page news. As it was, the action taken by the police was never reported, other than that they interviewed the laird in question and the manifestations thereafter ceased.

Tales with a basis of demonism have been encountered in every part of Scotland, and many of these seem spawned from the same culture, only the necessity for fitting them into a local background altering their construction. Dr. Forsyth, for instance, draws attention to the similarity between Hugh Millar's Cromarty story, "The Wild Wife", and a favourite tale in Strathspey called "The Legend of the Wife of Laggan".

There is another variation of the above which incorporates the main features of yet other legends. It is considered eligible for inclusion here because it concerns certain Grants of Glenmoriston. An added commendation is that it may now be seeing print for the first time.

THE DOWAGER OF DELFRUIN

The ruins of Delfruin Castle, once a turreted, grey freestone building, stand on a spit of rock at the edge of a little lochan which shines like a mirror in a long haugh of moorland running between two high ranges of hills. This haugh is called Faebuie, or the Yellow Moss. A lonely road connects the castle ruins with Kincraig to the east, while to the west were at one time several small estates and bien farm-towns.

The last owner and resident at Delfruin was an elderly dowager lady who had the most uncanny gift for detecting the weaknesses in human nature and making use of these to set the whole neighbourhood by the ears. Young lovers were parted soon after betrothal, and lifelong friends changed to bitter enemies by the skilful way she could weave her webs of calumnious lies, and had it not been for her exalted station in life there is little doubt that she would have been denounced as a witch to silence her wicked, spiteful tongue.

Ian MacGillivray, who lived with his wife on the estate nearest to Delfruin, was lucky enough to escape the Dowager's attention for several years, chiefly because she could find no flaw in his armour of decent living. Then one day, by the merest accident, she discovered a streak of jealousy in his nature. Shortly after this, hearing that the MacGillivrays had just become proud parents, she set about making the fullest, vilest use of her discovery.

With careful, feasible, and seemingly innocent insinuations, she played upon MacGillivray to such an extent that he ended up by taxing his wife with infidelity, even threatening to destroy the child. His treatment of her became so bad, in fact, that his wife, who before her marriage had been a Grant of Glenmoriston, wrote to her two brothers, imploring their aid, and a few days later they duly alighted at her gate.

On learning how matters stood, the brothers tried reasoning with the husband, with whom they had always been on the best of terms, but no amount of argument or cajolery could pierce the fog of jealousy shrouding his brain. At last the younger of the brothers was forced to suggest an unusual solution to the problem.

"It's obvious to me that your mind has been poisoned by this old woman you keep on telling us is your friend," he said quietly, "and it so happens that during my travels abroad, particularly in Middle Europe, I learned one sure way of dealing with a person of her kind."

"What do you mean by that?" asked MacGillivray.

"I mean that the three of us will pay a visit to this old beldame at Delfruin to-morrow. She is cunning, I know, but I propose to confront her with someone at least as clever as herself and, whatever else comes of the visit, we shall certainly arrive at the truth."

Next morning, in accordance with this plan, the husband and the two brothers set out for Delfruin Castle. The old lady received them with a great show of kindness, and when the brothers touched upon the subject in which they were chiefly interested she gave replies of seeming candour and much innocence. At last the younger brother lost patience with verbal fencing, and came directly to the point.

"You imply that my sister was unfaithful to her husband," he said bluntly, "and I now propose to put the matter up for proof to a mutual acquaintance who is greatly skilled at deciding such questions. Have I your permission to call him?"

Entirely unsuspecting his real intention, the dowager agreed; whereupon he took a blackened piece of charcoal from the fire-place and began tracing strange characters and symbols on the floor. As he did so, he kept muttering outlandish words in a foreign tongue.

The room in which they were gathered was a large chamber

with a row of narrow, unglazed windows looking out upon the loch. The day was calm and fine, the sky unblemished by cloud, but after the younger brother had been writing and murmuring for a time the waters of the lochan began to heave and swell until a great fleece of vapour rose from it, spreading out over the heavens and darkening the sun. His incantations continued unabated until at length all became aware of a tall dark figure, indefinite as the shadow thrown by a man in moonlight, standing in a corner of the room.

"Now, ask *him* if your wife has been faithful to you—only do it now and don't waste any time," said the younger brother to the husband.

Gaping towards the spectre, MacGillivray did as he was told.

"She has *always* been faithful," came the hollow-sounding reply; and as the words were uttered a great wave rose from the lochan and dashed against the windows.

"You brought *him* here, and now I'll thank you to send him away again," called out the dowager in alarm.

Before this could be replied to a great storm of wind and hail beat down on the castle, and the chamber's solid stone floor began to rise and fall like the deck of a ship in the teeth of a hurricane.

"He won't go without his bountith," shouted the younger brother in an effort to make himself heard above the noise of the storm. "Is there anyone in the castle you can spare?"

"I have a little orphan girl working for me," offered the dowager eagerly.

"No, I dare not touch her," said the shadow.

"Then why not take the old witch herself?" shouted the elder brother, as an even bigger wave smashed two of the windows and came flooding into the room.

"That's right, take her!" yelled MacGillivray, pointing at the castle's mistress.

"She is mine already, but her time is hardly out yet," was the sombre reply. Then the shadow looked directly at the last speaker. "The matter is settled," he went on. "From you, man of little faith, I will take my fee in a manner you would have little cared about an hour ago—but may now miss more."

With these words the shadow dispersed and vanished, and the sky grew clear and calm again.

MacGillivray, only too pleased to be quit of the castle, left without a word of recrimination. As he rode home he was filled with remorse at having doubted his wife, as well as being conscious of a great longing to take in his arms the child he had previously despised—but when he reached home he learned that the baby had died at approximately the same time as the shadow had vanished at Delfruin.

This loss, coupled with the knowledge of how the dowager had exploited his jealousy, kindled in the mind of Ian MacGillivray wild thoughts of revenge, but for three years following the appearance of the Black Shadow at Delfruin the grain produced in that part of the country was bleached and shrivelled, and he knew that no ordinary mortal would stand a chance in a battle of wits against such nameless forces as those surrounding the dowager.

Nevertheless, thoughts of squaring matters with the evil old woman kept recurring in his mind. This was markedly the case one night when, after a long day's hunting in the hills, he realized he was following the lonely road winding its way over the Yellow Moss, and passing close to the castle of Delfruin. The hour was late, and the moon, in its last quarter, had just topped the mountain on his right. This was partly veiled by strips of vapour rising in layers from the bog; an effect which added greatly to the moorland's air of ghostly unreality.

As he walked along, a solitary wayfarer, his surroundings assumed control of his thoughts and a strange new emotion took subtle hold of him. This was the queer, eerie conviction that he was in the vicinity of something unearthly and evil. He felt a chill creeping of the flesh and a prickling at the roots of his hair.

The moon clouded over; the night became suddenly black. His uneasiness increased until it finally brought him to a halt. Through the stillness whispered a faint sound like the rustling of a light air through the leaves of trees—then his whole being quivered with horror.

A shadowy female figure, gliding rather than walking, was coming up the road towards him. As it drew close he felt his heart racing; but to his intense relief the unspeakable wraith did not stop. It merely hesitated momentarily to call out in harassed tones:

"Is it possible to reach the hallowed ground at Kincraig kirk-yard before midnight?"

"No *living* being could," MacGillivray managed to reply, and this was acknowledged by a groan as the shape sped on out of view.

MacGillivray wanted to take to his heels and run, but the background whisper had increased in volume until it now contained a note of threat which fixed him to the ground more firmly than before.

Then he became aware of another figure, much taller but even less distinct than the first, bearing down upon him. This, somehow or other, gave the impression of a man on horseback.

"Is it possible to reach Kincraig kirkyard before midnight?" this apparition also asked.

"If that's a swift horse you're on, you might just manage it," answered MacGillivray, and the spectre vanished.

An instant later a shriek of torment and despair rang out in the distance. The clouds drifted clear of the moon and left it shining with a supernatural white light. The whispering grew faint, and changed to chuckling, devilish laughter.

MacGillivray was striving to force his trembling legs into movement when the wraith on horseback again came into view; this time clearly visible in the moonlight. As it drew level the watcher in the roadway almost choked with terror.

Drooping across the rider's saddle-bow lay the figure of a woman, and on either side of his horse trotted two great hounds. One of these was tugging at the woman's head; the other at her feet. As the terrible group passed the woman's face was clearly discernible, and, convulsed though it was with agony, Mac-Gillivray had no difficulty in recognizing the features of the Dowager of Delfruin.

An instant later the hellish cavalcade was gone, and the power of the watcher's legs returned.

He started running, totteringly at first, but with speed increasing at every stride, until at last he was covering that stretch of moorland road faster than man had ever done before. He passed the short branch road leading to Delfruin Castle at even greater speed, and it was only when he reached his own gates

that he realized he had subconsciously noted the castle was
in flames.

Next morning the charred remains of the Dowager were found
among the ruins, and Ian MacGillivray recalled the Dark
Shadow's words that day at the castle:

"*She is mine already, but her time is hardly out yet.*"

Now the hour of reckoning had come, and, coupled with what
he had witnessed on the night before, no further proof was
needed that a vengeance greater than any he could devise had
overtaken the evil old chatelaine. The grim reaper had garnered
that which he had sown, and at long last the devil had claimed
his own. . . .

An eerie tale of more recent date tells how the wicked Captain
MacPherson met a nameless fate on the last day of the year
1800. It is said that this laird, a man suspected of abominable
practices, was out hunting with some companions when they
were storm-bound and forced to spend the night at the bothy of
Gaik, many miles from the nearest habitation.

It seems that as the night wore on the Captain's companions
began to experience a growing dread. This changed to terror
when indescribable noises were heard coming from overhead.
One man said afterwards that it was as though a gigantic, form-
less "something" was slithering about on the roof, punctuating
its movement with loud bangs and a "swishing sound such as a
fishing-rod might make if used as a whip".

Of the bothy's occupants only the Captain was unperturbed.
He rose from his seat and made for the door.

"Oh, dinna open it, Laird, dinna open it," begged a ghillie,
grey with fear.

"Nonsense, man, there's nothing there that can harm *me*,"
said the Captain as he stepped outside.

Within the hut the men could hear the Captain speaking in
low tones, but were unable to distinguish what he said. They
could, however, make out every word of the bleating, goat-like
voice that answered him. This expressed anger and disappointment that the Captain had brought so few men.

It could be, of course, that the laird knew the noise on the
roof was caused by some perfectly natural agency, and assumed
the bleating voice himself to play upon his companions' ignorant

fears. Be that as it may, he returned to the same bothy a few nights after the occurrence, and was never again seen alive. When a search party went out to look for him they found the bothy demolished, crushed flat under an avalanche of snow, and the body of the wicked laird so mutilated as to be almost unrecognizable.

Tales in the demoniac genre have been little known in Strathspey during the past century, but place names, such as the "Cave of the Hellish Man" in Abernethy, suggest that at one time they were more plentiful. There is, however, one legend of particular interest to myself, not only because the locale can be viewed from the window of the room in which these lines are being written, but also because it has a neatness of construction not always found in tales of this kind. It begins in the Parish of Cromdale about 300 years ago:

THE LADY OF CASTLE CLASH

At the time of this happening the Allt Neat was a turbulent river (though now no more than a sizeable burn) that wound its way peacefully enough through the high moorland of Dava until forced to make the steep drop down to the Spey. Here impatience got the better of it, causing it to cut its way through peat and limestone with such ferocity that it carved a deep gash in the hillside, so narrow at one point that the hunted deer could leap it without difficulty and a man could bridge it by edging along the intertwining branches of the trees growing on either side.

The rushing river itself was hidden by greenery and black shadow, but its voice could be heard moaning and wailing like an unshriven spirit lamenting the imprisonment of the tomb.

This grim place was called the Clash (ravine), and to look down into it gave one a creepy feeling. The sun never penetrated the gloom of its depths, yet in the twilit lower reaches the mouths of caverns were discernible, and it was even possible to glimpse dividing waters as they boiled over rock and fall.

At no great distance from the ravine stood Castle Clash, the home of Captain Ian Alanach, a Grant who had recently escaped from Cromwell's Roundheads at Worcester and had returned with a wife; met and married no one knew where.

This lady, though lovely to look at, was a strange sort of person, and although the Captain's simple clansfolk respected her because she was the Laird's wife they were also afraid of her, largely because of her liking for lonely walks along stretches of the Clash that even the boldest of the local men shunned whenever possible. There was also an unearthly *something* about her which filled them with awe.

One day, for no apparent reason, the lady's whole manner underwent a change. Colour came into her pale cheeks, a new light shone in her eyes, and she began to show the servants little acts of kindness that took them all by surprise. To her own personal maid she was particularly gracious, braiding her hair, dressing her in a new green silken gown, and finally taking her as a companion when she went walking.

Despite these attentions, however, Shona, the maid, was still nervous, especially when her mistress guided her footsteps towards the Clash one evening just as the sun was going down, and then invited her to come right up to the ravine's edge.

The poor girl was terror-stricken and refused to obey, whereupon her mistress, with a demoniacal glare in her eyes and a strength altogether out of keeping with one of her delicate build, began dragging her in the dreaded direction. Shona was almost fainting when she heard a masculine voice speak, and saw a man in a green plaid and kilt standing just behind them. The lady stared at him.

"When I agreed to accept a surety for you I insisted that she come of her own free will," the stranger addressed her sternly. "In any case, this is a *good* girl—what possible use could she be to me?"

The rage died in the lady's face, to be replaced by a look of resignation. She released Shona and advanced to the edge of the precipice. Here she paused, took the keys from her girdle and threw them towards the maid. As they landed on a granite boulder the stranger took the lady by the wrist and both disappeared over the rim of the ravine.

For a time Shona stood rooted in terror, then she stooped to pick up the keys. These had sunk into the granite as though it had been putty, and when lifted left a clear impression on the otherwise smooth rock.

The girl staggered home and told her master what had happened; but though he and his men searched for many days no trace of the missing lady could be found.

The years passed, Captain Alanach died, there was no heir, and the castle sank into ruin; the stones latterly being used to build a new farm-town, called Balnaclash.[1] The story of the Lady of Castle Clash dimmed to legend and might have been completely forgotten had not a strange new happening again brought it to the fore.

One Donald Beg Rose, working for the lady who owned the new steading, was sent to catch fish for the household in the spating waters of the Allt Neat. He was successful in this, but, knowing his mistress was mean enough to claim *all* the fish, he concealed part of his catch under a juniper bush. His employer, however, too shrewd and suspicious to be easily deceived, refused to believe that the basket contained the whole of his catch.

"It's the devil himself I call to witness that every fish I took is here," insisted Donald Beg; then at the first opportunity he hurried off to collect his spoils and take them home to his aged mother.

But when he reached the juniper bush there was no longer any fish there; nothing in fact but a scale-speckled track, suggesting that some animal had found the trout and dragged them off to its lair.

No more pleased at being robbed than his mistress had been, Donald Beg followed the trail of the stolen fish, not hesitating even when it led within the towering walls of the Clash.

The ravine narrowed and grew dark, though the sun was still high in the heavens, but Donald Beg's heart was as big as his body was small, and he kept on until he found himself at the mouth of a large cave. Stepping cautiously forward he peered within; then gasped with astonishment at what he saw.

On either side of the entrance lay a huge hound, while within the cave's depths he could see a lady seated on a chair by a table; both pieces of furniture made of iron and red with rust. On the table lay his fish, while from the lady's right ankle dangled a rusty iron chain.

[1] Not the present farm of this name.

"Who may you be, m'leddy, and what are you doing here?" asked Donald Beg.

"I am the Lady of Castle Clash," was the resigned reply. "Once I sold my soul to the devil, just as you called him to witness a while back—but so far it is only I who have been made to pay the penalty."

"I'll take you away with me," said Donald Beg.

"Captain Alanach did that once, but to what purpose?" sighed the lady. "No, you must give up the fish you denied your mistress in the name of my jailer, and make your escape while there is still time. See, the dogs are awake and rising."

"It's steel in their bellies I'll give them," said the dauntless Donald Beg, whipping out his dirk.

"No, there is a better way," said the lady, picking up two of the fish and throwing them towards the hounds. "Go while they are eating, and never come back this way again."

Realizing at last that he had been tackling forces too strong for him, Donald Beg did as he was told.

That was the last ever seen of the Lady of Castle Clash. Shortly after this an earthquake rent the ravine apart, changing its precipitous sides into gentle slopes, now clad in birch, larch and pine.

That tale also has its variants in different parts of Scotland, and must be very much older than the period allotted to it in the above version. Only a very considerable cataclysm of nature could have altered the Clash in the manner described, and there is no supporting evidence in this locality to suggest that an earthquake of the requisite intensity has been experienced in this part of Strathspey within the past 1,000 years. A minor earthquake was felt here in 1816, but apart from the curious belief that it was responsible for several children being stricken by paralysis, it does not appear to have done much material damage.

It was in this Clash, near Darraid, that a fugitive Earl of Huntly once took refuge, and a hand-painted sign-post near Lyne MacGregor now unobtrusively directs visitors who have come out from Grantown in search of the Earl of Huntly's Cave.

One strange thing about this Clash legend is that in this land of long memories there is no tradition of a castle ever having stood there, although there are some vague and hazy references to an old "fort" having occupied a site near Huntly's Cave. It is also significant that I did not pick up the tale in the environs of Cromdale. I heard it one day quite by chance from a man in Newtonmore. He told me that his great-grandparents came from Achnarrow, in the parish of Cromdale, and through which the Clash runs for part of its way. It was they who had handed the tale down to their children.

So far as its application to Strathspey is concerned, this legend also may now be seeing print for the first time.

CHAPTER XI

GRANTS AND MIGRANTS

Proud record of a name – Associations with the Black Watch – The Strathspey Highlanders – The Kilted Marines – The beautiful Lady Anne – Election fever – The Clan Grant raid on Elgin – Sergeant Roy – Ian Mor of Duthil – Ian-na-lite of Cromdale – Ian Mor of Kincardine – Ian Mor's fight with the English champion – " Grants of the Trough " – World population of Grants – The Grants of Man- chester – Dickens' Cheeryble Brothers.

I T may seem a rash statement to make, but I honestly believe that no other surname in Britain has been carried to prominence so frequently as that of Grant. There is scarcely an aspect of creditable human activity, be it in the fields of military service, science, commerce, the professions or the arts, where bearers of the name have not attained pre-eminence.

There has been a Field-Marshal Grant, an Admiral Grant, an Air-Marshal Grant, and Generals Grants by the score. The clan have even provided the United States of America with a President, and there has also been a Grant President of the Royal Academy. In foreign, non-English-speaking coun- tries their talents have brought them nobility and honours typified by those bestowed upon Charles Grant, Vicomte de Vaux.

In the military field a feature of interest was the clan's long association with the Black Watch. A Grant of Ballindalloch raised one of the original companies of this regiment, and over a continuous period of 150 years it was never without at least one officer of the name of Grant; a long succession of gallant gentlemen who added lustre to both unit and clan. It is because of this association that the Grants wear the Black Watch *breacan* as their Hunting Tartan, and this is also recognized as the Dis- trict Tartan of Strathspey as a whole.

For some years now Strathspey's local regiment has been the Seaforth Highlanders, but the district has also had affiliations with other formations; now too often forgotten. First of these was the Grant Fencibles, levied by the Good Sir James when Britain went to war with France in 1793. This volunteer battalion was recruited for service within Scotland only, but Sir James later raised another regiment for general service. This was the Strathspey Highlanders, or 97th Foot. I cannot say with certainty whether they were the first, or only, kilted Marines, but they served in this capacity for several months with Lord Howe's fleet, after which they were split up and drafted, the two flank companies (the battalion's best) going to the Black Watch; ther about to embark for the West Indies.

For those who consider the Battle of Mulroy (1689) as being the last occasion a clan went on the warpath on its own account, it may come as something of a surprise to learn that the Grants last mustered and marched as a clan with aggressive intent as late as 1820.

This happened when Lewis Ogilvie-Grant, Earl of Seafield, was staying at Grant Lodge (now the County Library) in Elgin; his sisters, Lady Anne and Lady Penuel, sharing residence with him. It was election time, with the Earl of Seafield championing the candidature of Mr. Farquharson of Finzean, and Lord Fife that of General Duff. The townspeople of Elgin favoured the last-named, and election fever reached such a pitch that the Lady Anne and her sister dared not venture out into the streets without running the risk of being grossly insulted.

Confinement to the well-appointed Lodge was but little hardship to the easy-going Penuel, but to the proud, high-spirited Anne the situation was intolerable; especially when the excited mob surrounded the house and prevented anyone from entering or leaving.

This was more than the imperious Lady Anne could stand. Of great beauty and accomplishments, she was idolized by the people of Strathspey, and she knew that the slightest appeal to them would bring aid in the present emergency. She so arranged matters that a groom was smuggled out of the house, first to mingle with the crowd and then set off hot-foot to Strathspey. Being a Nethybridge man, that was where he went first to disseminate his news.

It was Sunday and, the living at the Parish Church being temporarily vacant, an open-air service in Gaelic, attended by a large congregation, was being held at Straanbeg. The messenger made straight for Sergeant Roy, a Peninsular War veteran whose word carried some weight in the parish.

The psalm was being sung when the minister noticed a strange stirring among the worshippers and saw them gradually begin to form into small groups. The sweet cadence of the singing, mingling with the melody of rippling waters and sighing wind, dropped almost to nothingness as men left their places in the lines of worshippers and made their way out of hearing in answer to signals from beckoning friends.

"What has happened?" one man asked Sergeant Roy.

"Grant Lodge is beseiged and Lady Anne is in danger," was the old soldier's reply. "The clan is to march on Elgin; I'll tell you the rest as we go along."

"Is it to be sword and gun?" asked a young man eagerly.

"No, only cromachs and staves," said Roy, "and a fine long walk to carry them.'

Smoke rose high from the beacons on the two Craigellachies, and 150 men mustered in Nethybridge alone. They were given counsel as to their behaviour from Captain Grant of Birchfield, then, mindful that it was the Sabbath, they marched quietly away about six p.m.

At Old Spey Bridge, Grantown, they were joined by men from the Braes of Castle Grant; these armed with muskets and swords. It was dark when they reached Cromdale, and here they were greeted with the news that the Cromdale men had left some hours before. The main body reached Aberlour about midnight, and were partaking of refreshment there when the clock struck twelve.

"That's the Sabbath away," called out one man. "Strike up a tune, Peter Bain."

The piper was only too willing to oblige, and to the strains of "The Haughs of Cromdale" the marchers were soon on the move again. When they reached the rock at the lower Craigellachie they paused for a moment to shout their slogan, the stillness of the night being shattered by their resounding yell: "Stand fast, Craigellachie!"

The Cromdale men were the first to arrive in Elgin, reaching the town about three a.m. Then came the Nethybridge contingent, followed by the men of Duthil. In all, they amounted to a force of about 600 strong. They were met on the outskirts by

THE OPEN
STRATH

With Cromdale
Hills and
Cairngorm
Mountains

some well-wishers, and as the reason for their presence was to quell trouble rather than to provoke it they were guided to Grant Lodge by the quietest roads possible.

This did not mean that their progress was undisputed. One old Elgin wifie tried to bar their advance single-handed by stepping out before them yelling:

"The Whigs and Lord Fife for ever!"

One of the men, annoyed by her screaming in his ear, was pushing her out of the way when her heel caught in the gutter and she fell. From her seat on the ground, however, she still continued to shriek her defiance.

"Well done, *Cailleach*," called out the lines of men as they passed, stirred to admiration by her courage.

With pipes skirling, Grant Lodge was reached as the town was coming to full life. It was a tense situation, for although the Highlanders had been warned to practise restraint it needed only the right sort of incident to apply the match that would set their tempers alight. Fortunately, the citizens of Elgin realized this, and remembering what the men from the hills had done when under the leadership of the Wolf of Badenoch, they were careful not to supply undue provocation.

All that day and throughout the following night the Strathspey men remained; entertained in great fashion by the lady they had come to succour. When the second day dawned they marched away again. The raid had achieved its purpose without bloodshed. The people of Elgin were now aware of the wrath their undisciplined actions could bring upon them, and when the Lady Anne next went out walking it was to be greeted with signs of marked respect.

The Sergeant Roy just referred to was one of the soldiers who helped to carry Sir John Moore from the field at Corunna, and he was also present when General Abercrombie received his fatal wound at Alexandria. The General, in great pain, was being carried to a waiting boat when Sir John MacDonald slipped a blanket under his head.

"Thanks, that is a comfort—what is it, John?" asked the wounded commander.

"Only a soldier's blanket, Sir Ralph," was the reply.

"Which soldier's?"

"Duncan Roy Grant's, of the 42nd," said Sir John.

I

"Then make sure he gets it back again and does not have to go blanketless to-night," was the considerate command, ere the speaker was moved from litter to death-bed.

Moore and Abercrombie were Sergeant Roy's heroes. In his often-expressed view they were more able generals than Wellington.

Several notable Grants have borne the name *Ian Mor*, or Big John. Ian Mor of Duthil is remembered for having carried his fatally-wounded Chief from the field after a battle with raiding MacKintoshes. This was in the sixteenth century. He took his injured leader to the church at Duthil, where he died shortly after arrival and was buried in the churchyard. In this way was established the family burial ground, retained in constant use until the interment of the Countess Caroline, as already mentioned.

Ian Mor of Cromdale was also known as *Iain-na-lite*, or John of the Porridge. He was a man of great strength, yet, strangely enough, it is his encounter with porridge rather than human adversary that is best recalled to-day. There are several versions of how his name came to be associated with this dish, but the one I like best is the following.

Ian returned to Cromdale after a carousal at Inverness to find the Figgat Fair in progress. He had spent all his money and was desperately hungry, so that when passing a huckster's stall he was more than interested to hear the vendor of gew-gaws offer a substantial prize in money to any man who could eat ten basins of his porridge in ten minutes. In fact, this sounded to Ian Mor very much like a gift from the gods; and it was only when he took up the challenge that he discovered there was a catch in it.

The porridge was served boiling hot and, as everyone knows, this food takes a long time to cool. No artificial means being allowed for lowering the dish's temperature, and considering the speed with which it had to be consumed, the showman was confidant of retaining his coin. To make absolutely certain on this point, however, he also stipulated that no spoon or other utensil was to be used. Nothing daunted, Ian Mor still decided to go on.

When the first basin was filled Ian quickly ran two fingers round the rim of the dish, scooping out the porridge where it had been in contact with the sides, and thus been lowered well below boiling point. In this way he continued until he had consumed the whole ten basins with more than a minute to spare. As the disgusted showman was paying over the prize-money Ian Mor noticed that there was still some porridge left in the pot. He asked the showman what he intended to do with it.

"Don't tell me you'd be willing to eat that also?" the latter gasped.

"That I would," assured Ian Mor, "so long as there was no hurry attached to it, and I'd have time to enjoy it properly."

But the greatest Ian Mor of them all was the one who hailed from Kincardine. He was a natural son of the Grant Chief, *Ian-nan-bard-roy* (Red John the Poet) and a daughter of the Baron of Kincardine. Of great strength and stature, he was cast in the ancient heroic mould and his deeds of valour provided themes for many bardic tales and songs.

Once, when arriving in Edinburgh to wait upon his father, he found that the Grant Chief, together with his kinsman, the MacKintosh of MacKintosh, were lodged as prisoners in the Castle gaol. Ian Mor, having tried to make contact with the prisoners without success, was walking disconsolately down the High Street when he found a large concourse of Edinburgh townsfolk evidently in a state of high excitement. On inquiring the cause of this, he learned that a renowned English "Billy" was in town and had defeated every champion the Scottish capital could put up against him.

On hearing this Ian Mor walked over to where the City Provost and his magistrates were standing. He asked them what his prize would be if he defeated the Englishman.

"Anything that lies in our power to grant," was the Provost's reply.

"I would ask no more than I am able to carry unaided from the Castle," said Ian Mor.

At that time the Castle was a sparsely-furnished fortress, and as the magistrates could not think of anything of great value that one man could bear off they willingly agreed to Ian Mor's terms. The English pugilist was then called upon the scene.

The Englishman was greatly skilled in fisticuffs, an art of which Ian Mor knew nothing, and he was also an exponent of several styles of wrestling, of which the Strathspey man knew even less. Realizing all this from his opponent's stance, the Englishman anticipated an easy victory and rushed forward to administer

the *coup de grâce* without delay. But whatever Ian Mor lacked
in science, he more than made up for in agility and strength.
Evading the full force of the Englishman's blows, he darted in
suddenly and seized him by neck and crutch. The professional
prize-fighter was a heavy, powerful man, but that did not
prevent Ian Mor from raising him high in the air and dashing him with such force to the ground that he was instantly
killed.

The city magistrates were delighted at the honour of Edinburgh being upheld in such spectacular fashion, and all accompanied Ian Mor to the Castle to ensure that he would obtain his
reward. Arrived there, he demanded that the Lairds of Grant
and MacKintosh be handed over to him. These two were also
big men, and one of the magistrates reminded Ian Mor that he
could only take away what he could carry unaided.

" I am not forgetting that," said Ian Mor, as he took the Laird
of Grant upon his back. " Now bring out the MacKintosh and
put him on top of my father."

Thus laden, Ian Mor walked through the gates to freedom.

This Ian Mor, later called John of Culcabock, had a notable
career and finished his life as a great landowner. His father
bestowed upon him the lands of Urquhuart in Glenmoriston,
thus forming the Glenmoriston branch of the clan, and he also
held estates in Carron, Wester Elchies and Kinchirdy, in Strathspey, as well as lands in the Western Highlands.

He divorced his first wife, Isabella Innes, and then married
Agnes Fraser, a granddaughter of the Fourth Lord Lovat. This
union was within the forbidden degree of consanguinity, but a
dispensation was granted by the Pope (1544) absolving him from
the crime of incest and granting legitimacy to any children born
of the marriage. A son of the union, Patrick, from whom the
Grants of Glenmoriston are known as Clan Patrick, succeeded to
most of his estates, although Carron and Wester Elchies went to
two illegitimate sons, John Roy and James.

Not all Grants received their surname at the baptismal font,
or even adopted it from choice, as witness the case of the *Sliochd-
an-amair* or "Race of the Trough ".

Local tradition connects their origin with the Grant Chief
known as *Seumais-nan-Creach* (James of the Forays), acting in
conjunction with the Earl of Huntly. We are told that the

Gordon Baron of Brackly entertained some members of the Clan Chattan and was basely murdered by them, whereupon Huntly resolved to avenge his clansman. This he did by summoning aid from the Chief of Grant, also Brackly's kinsman, and proceeding against the Farquharsons in Strathdee, a prominent branch of Clan Chattan.

A terrible massacre of the Deeside men followed, and the Laird of Grant was reminded of the grim happening when he visited Huntly about a year later. When they had finished eating a particularly good dinner, Huntly said to him : " Come and I'll show you something I'll swear you've never seen before."

James of the Forays accompanied his host out to the courtyard, where a long trough was placed near a wall. The remains of the feast were emptied into this, then a huntsman blew a blast on his silver whistle.

At this signal a hatch was raised in the doorway of a nearby building, and from it rushed a mob of yelling, screaming children, biting and scratching in their fight to get at the trough and its contents.

"Whelps of the Farquharsons," explained Huntly callously. "I have been sore put to it to feed the brats during the past year."

The Laird of Grant was horrified.

"My sword helped to make them orphans, and it is scarcely fair that you should carry all the burden of maintaining them," he said to his host. "I'll tell you what : I'll take all the children on one side of the trough, and you can have those on the other. In this way we can share responsibility for their upkeep, like we did in the task of slaying their fathers."

This was agreed upon, and when James of the Forays got back to Strathspey he divided his adopted charges among his clansfolk, leaving orders that they were to be known as Grants from that day on. This command was obeyed, and Clan Chattan children whose fathers had borne proud names such as MacHamish and MacFinlay Roy were scornfully referred to as "Grants of the Trough". Some of their descendants are still in Strathspey, and can generally be recognized by the incidence of their Farquharson Christian names. They have no cause for shame. They stem from a clan whose honourable record is surpassed by none.

It would be difficult to estimate the world-population of Grants at the present day, but I think it would be safe to say that for every hundred of the name still to be found in Strathspey, tens of thousands are now living in other parts of Britain and the Commonwealth generally. I have been given to understand that there are over 20,000 in the United States of America alone, and using this as a basis for calculation their total number in all countries cannot be far short of 100,000.

To examine the reasons for such an exodus, and to learn something of how at least one family of Grants fared when they left their home, let us glance at the story of William, of Elchies of Knockando, who left Strathspey in 1783.

William Grant was a professional cattle-drover, that is to say, he bought in cattle from surrounding crofts and then drove them to the markets in the south for sale. The years 1782-83 have come down to us as "The Pease Years", when the country was dangerously close to the famine level and beasts were thin and ill fed. By the time William got his herd to Perth they were little more than skin and bone, and no buyer would look at them. The same thing happened when he pressed on to Falkirk, about thirty miles farther on.

This placed the drover in a most precarious position, but his was not the temperament to give in easily and, hoping that he might strike some good wayside grazing the farther south he went, he continued on over the border into England.

Carlisle refused to look at his stock, and before he got down into Lancashire many of his beasts had fallen by the wayside. When they came to the valley of the Irwell William and his family were faced with starvation, but, as his son, William, afterwards wrote:

"As we passed along the old road, we stopped for a short time on the Park estate, to view the valley. My father exclaimed: 'What a beautiful valley! It reminds me of Speyside, even if the Irwell is not so large as the River Spey.' Turning to me he then said: 'This is paradise. Here I would like to have my home.'"

That night William called his family around him and they all knelt down beside their cart to pray that God's mercy would be shown to the children at least by having bread sent them. Next morning, two gentlemen who were out shooting came upon the family, and hearing of their plight prevailed upon Mrs. Grant to accept two sovereigns.

Grizel Grant (who had been a MacKintosh before her marriage) was convinced that this was a direct answer to her prayer; and it is a fact that they never knew actual want from that day onwards. William sold his few remaining beasts, and they continued on into Manchester. Here he applied to a Mr. Dinwiddie, a fellow-Scot who had known him in his more prosperous days, and this gentleman placed him in employment at his mill, not far from Bury. More than this, he articled William's two sons, William and James, as apprentices, and, when he was fully skilled, offered to take William, Jun., into partnership.

Young William, however, had other ideas. Here is what he, himself, had to say on the matter:

"I declined this offer, and commenced business for myself on a small scale, assisted by my brothers, John, Daniel and Charles, and removed to Bury where I was most successful; and in the course of a few years (1800) I removed to Manchester and commenced printing in partnership with my brothers.

"My brother Daniel commenced travelling through the north of England and almost to every market town in Scotland. In 1806 we purchased the print works belonging to Sir Robert Peel, situated at Ramsbottom. In 1812 we purchased Nuttal factory, where, in consequence of the death of Mr. Alsop, the work-people had long been short of employment, and were very destitute. We ordered the manager to get new machinery of the first-rate construction, and greatly extended the building; and before we began to spin or manufacture, we clothed the whole of the hands at our expense; prepared an entertainment for them, and observed that the interests of masters and servants are bound up together; that there are reciprocal duties to perform, that no general or admiral could be brave unless he was supported by his men; that we knew how to reward merit, and would give constant employment and liberal wages to all our faithful servants; and I am happy to say that they, as well as those at our printing establishment, with very few exceptions, have conducted themselves with great propriety.

"In 1818 we purchased Springside, and in 1827 we purchased the Park Estate, and erected a monument to commemorate our father's first visit to this valley, on the very spot where he and I stood admiring the beautiful scenery below. . . ."

That extract comes from a letter William Grant, Jun., sent to a friend in 1839, but two separate incidents in the lives of the brothers, William and Daniel, may help to picture them even more clearly.

Once the director of a well-known Liverpool firm, finding his business threatened with disaster, came to Daniel and asked for a loan of from £6,000 to £8,000. Daniel immediately signed a cheque for £10,000, and would not hear of security.

"Pooh, it's nothing," he cried, waving aside all safeguards. "It's a thing of honour; pay when you can, pay when you can."

When James Naysmith was starting in business he had an introduction to the Grants. At their house in Morley Street the first thing Daniel did was introduce him to his "noble brother, William", as he always affectionately called him. Some questions as to Naysmith's age and prospects then followed.

"How much money have you to start with?" asked Daniel.

"Sixty-three pounds," was the reply.

"H'm, that wouldn't get you very far when the first pay-day came round," said Daniel. "But, don't be disheartened. When you have to meet your first wage bill you'll find £500 paid into your credit at Cannon Street, and, as I consider you a gentleman, there will be no need for security."

One business rival wrote a pamphlet making a scurrilous and libellous attack upon the Grant brothers. William was in company when he was shown it. His only comment was: "The man who wrote that will be sorry some day."

This came to the ears of the libeller who, not unnaturally, took it as a threat. It can readily be imagined what he felt like a few years later when, faced with bankruptcy, he realized William Grant was his chief creditor.

"What can I do?" he moaned to a friend.

"I'd advise you to go to Mr. Grant and tell him exactly how you're placed," was the counsel given.

"But I daren't—how could I possibly expect any favour from him?" cried the unhappy man.

"I know Mr. Grant better than you do," said his friend, "and, in any case, it won't cost you anything to try."

In due course, the libeller went in desperation to see William.

He begged that he would sign a stay of foreclosure in company with other creditors.

"I have the paper here; if only you will add your signature," he said.

William held out his hand for the document, wrote something on it, and passed it back again.

"You once wrote a pamphlet about me, and I said then that you'd be sorry," he remarked quietly.

The man glanced at the paper, expecting to find "slanderer", or some such entry written upon it, but all he could see was the signature he had asked for.

"I was not threatening you—only expressing a firm conviction," went on William with a reassuring smile. "I guessed that some day you would know me better, and feel ashamed of the attack you made upon my brother and me. Don't lose heart. I'll stand by you and your family in your hour of need. No, don't waste time in thanks. I'm a busy man; good day."

I consider these glimpses of Grants out of their native Strathspey setting most illuminating, but if anyone would like to appreciate them yet more fully, then all they have to do is read their Dickens. For William and Daniel Grant are the models he drew upon for his sketch of the "Cheeryble Brothers".

Truly noble and great-hearted gentlemen; worthy ambassadors of the land whence they came.

CHAPTER XII

DOWNSTREAM

Cromdale – At the Carn Lethen – Entry in a Visitor's Book – Castle Grant – The ancient barony – The fight at the Figgat Fair – Ballindalloch – The Castle Stripe – The MacPherson Grants – The Spey at Carron – The plan of Captain Shanks – Aberlour – The brawling burn – A notable court case – The lower Craigellachie – Telford's Bridge – The long strath ends.

CROMDALE is a large parish, stretching on the one hand from the Braes of Moray to the crest of the Cromdale Hills, and from the Lettochs and Dalvey to the Bridge of Brown road and Grantown-on-Spey on the other, but the village of the same name is no more than a wayside hamlet, and not particularly pleasing to the eye. This lack of charm, however, is more than made up for in the parish as a whole, with surroundings comprising beautiful woodlands, rich farmlands, and dominating hills. The eastern parish boundary, in fact, runs for several miles without ever dropping below 2,000 feet.

Etymologists all follow one another faithfully in assuring us that "Cromdale" is a composite word coming from the Gaelic *crom*, "crooked', and the Norse *dale*, "haugh". My own view is that this derivation may not be quite so exact as it appears at first glance. *Crom*, or *Bel*, is also the very old Druidic name for the Sun God, and we should remember that the ancient name for Strathspey was *Griannus*, or Land of the Sun.

In the tenth century the parish was noted as *Skirmaluac* (District of St. Maluac), but it must certainly have had a name before this saint's time, and when one of the early Cymric poets, writing in the ninth century, speaks of "Delcrom in the Northern Pictish land", we must admit the possibility of the name having another, and much older, origin. *Delcrom* is entirely Gaelic and means "Place of the Sun God".

A final argument against the "crooked haugh" derivation is that although the river bends and curves here it is not running *through* the haugh when it does so, but along the western edges of it. In other words, the real Haugh of Cromdale is the stretch of alluvial land between the river and the Cromdale Hills, and while the river is crooked enough along one of its boundaries, the haugh itself is as straight as any I know.

The highest point on the Cromdale Hills is Carn Eachie (2,315 feet). The second highest, the old Carn Lethen, was used in Druidical days as a *carntyne*, or ritual cairn fire. In 1898 a Jubilee Cairn was built at the expense of the older Carn Lethen, and the ancient stones of the latter are now left strewn over a large area. This Jubilee Cairn has a cavity built into it which contains a visitor's book and pencil, kept weather-proof by being enclosed in an empty cocoa-tin.

For the most part the entries in this book are factual and unimaginative, but occasionally one comes across items that make the toil of climbing to the hill-top worth while. Here is one such I read about nine years ago. It was written by a woman visitor from the south.

" Pinned against a steep hill-side by a villainous sun, and grilled as though I was in a frying-pan, I have survived the onslaughts of millions of the most hellish insects, and at last achieved what I set out to do—reach the top of this blasted mountain. I MUST BE MAD! "

There are, of course, attractions other than reading a visitor's book to be met with at the end of this climb. I have twice reached the cliff-like rampart where the cairn is perched to disturb the solitude of a gloriously-plumaged Golden Eagle, and on each occasion I was just in time to see him take off into the wind. A minute of hovering, treating me to a detailed view of the white barring on his pinions, then the Lord of the Air went wheeling upwards in great spirals before disappearing in the direction of Dava Moor.

On yet another occasion I witnessed a remarkable tableau-effect presented by creamy-white, large horned sheep, posing pyramid fashion on the steep, rocky face of the cairn rampart. Descendants of domestic sheep imported to the area over two hundred years ago, these creatures are now quite wild and as agile as any chamois. This particular band must have come from the Cairngorms, and my arrival on the scene evidently reminded them that it was time to return there, for with a grace

it was a joy to behold, they darted over the skyline, vanishing in the twinkling of an eye.

In the south-west corner of the parish, standing in its rich policies of meadow, field and beautiful woodland, is Castle Grant, home of the chiefly house of Freuchie Grants for hundreds of years, but at present unoccupied. Its first known version, termed *Ballycaistell*, or Castle of the Pass, was built in the fifteenth century, and was later known as Castle Freuchie (*Caisteal Fraoghaire*—or Castle in the Heather). These two names were quite descriptive of the castle in those early times, because the surroundings then were very different from what they are to-day, heath and bog being the main features in an area now covered by a great variety of trees, including pines and larches upwards of two hundred years old.

So many lairds made additions and improvements to the original buildings that it is difficult to give an exact date for the castle in its present form, but some of the original features (such as Babette's tower) have been retained, although hard to distinguish from the bald mass of masonry which Queen Victoria affected to mistake for a factory.

If ever a dwelling-place was two-faced, then this one is. Viewed from the north-west front, with its four main storeys and row of attics, Castle Grant is completely featureless and devoid of all expression, architectural or otherwise. All one really notes is uniform windows, arranged in strictly symmetrical rows, that are a direct negation of imagination in any shape or form. On the south-east side, however, where two protruding wings hem in a courtyard approached by a flight of steps, the total effect is not unpleasing. In these wings the kitchen and other domestic offices were housed, while under the courtyard and ground floors of the building were stabling for horses and a byre for milking-cows.

The last tenants to actually live in the castle were Indian troops during the Second World War. In the bitterly cold winter of 1939 they tried to introduce a little warmth and comfort into their lives by baking a few chupatties on the wooden ground floor, and this resulted in a series of fires. While not destroying the castle, these did not improve its appearance, and when the kitchen wing was burnt out about seven years ago, the fate of the castle as a future family residence was apparently sealed.

The entrance hall, main staircase and dining-room are still furnished, museum fashion, with the muskets and petronnels of the Grant Fencibles, all gleaming and looking ready for instant use, and some interesting paintings, ranging from portraits by the inimitable Waitt to works of greater artistic value. Above the stair-landing is a beautifully executed portrait of Charles Grant, Vicomte de Vaux. This is ten feet in length and is presumed to have been the work of the royal painter at the court of the French king. Some of the paintings are no more than well-produced copies, but I should say that others, like "An Encampment" by Bassau, are originals and worthy of appreciative consideration.

Visitors to Grantown need experience little difficulty in looking over Castle Grant. Mr. Templeton, who lives in the gate-lodge nearest the town, is a charming, willing and informative guide.

The walks within the castle policies are many and varied. The trees here range from blue cedar, Sitka spruce, larch and native pine to most of the shady deciduous varieties, including ash, beech, oak and a delightful avenue of limes. It is said that the limes were planted by an ultra-civilized laird who wanted a place close to the castle where he could indulge in a little gentle exercise without exposing his complexion to the rigours of the sun.

Cromdale was once owned by the MacDuff Earls of Fife, but in the fourteenth century they resigned it to the Crown and it was later bestowed upon the Nairn Family, one of whom was called Baron of Cromdale. It was from a Nairn that Sir Ludovick Grant purchased the barony in 1609, and was later granted a royal charter with power to found a burgh here.

At one time the Grant chiefs had great plans for Cromdale, then much more populous than it is now. It had a court-house, prison and school, close to where the Mains farm now stands, together with shops of various kinds, and was also the venue of the annual Figgat Fair. This last, while bestowing considerable prestige on the new burgh was also the cause of its downfall. At this market a fight broke out between rival factions of Grants, some of whom were old residents and the others new-comers introduced by the laird from farther up the strath.

The result of this fracas was that the defeated incomers left the locality and set up new homes near the gates of Castle Grant, placing themselves directly under the Chief's protection. This impromptu settlement on his doorstep was an eyesore to Sir Ludovick, and it was probably a desire to remove these displaced persons elsewhere that caused him to draw up his plans for Grantown in the first instance. In any case, a new, distinctive little town in lovely surroundings sprang into being, while Cromdale slipped back into the rural anonymity its inhabitants still prefer.

The Haughs of Cromdale have been rendered famous by a pipe-tune of the same name, and the fact that a battle was fought on them in 1690. The pipe-tune was given its place in history when the wounded Piper Findlater played it at the storming of the Heights of Dargai (1897). The battle has been dealt with by so many historians, myself included, that I do not propose to say any more about it here; other than that it really was a battle, and not at all the featureless rout that some writers would have us believe.[1]

Like almost anywhere else in Strathspey, the village and parish of Advie, about seven miles downstream from Cromdale, is rich in Druidic relics and other pre-historic remains, but what I have always considered most interesting about it is the multiplicity of roles it plays in the matter of boundaries. Until about a hundred years ago it was the boundary between the Gaelic and English speaking population (Gaelic then being regularly preached in Cromdale Church), as well as between the parishes of Cromdale and Inveravon. At the present day it still marks the boundary between the counties of Moray and Banff; the Seafield and Ballindalloch estates; the Buchan and Moray "Nations" at Aberdeen University; and forms the demarcation line between Upper and Lower Strathspey.

After leaving Advie there is a gradual closing in of the rolling land on either side of the river, with sloping hill-side fields more and more taking the place of the flat bottom-lands farther upstream. When Ballindalloch is reached this alteration in topography is quite marked; not least by the change in vegetation due to the lowering of altitude.

This is particularly noticeable at the high-sprung stone bridge spanning the ravine over the River Avon, for here the banks are lined with beech, ash and other deciduous trees whose foliage,

[1] See p. 106 *In the Steps of the Clansmen.*

even on the sunniest days give an impression of everlasting twilight.

To get the full impact of this bridge it is, perhaps, best to go over it for the first time in a motor-coach. The effect is truly startling, as the road beyond is no more than a shelf cut out of the towering rock face of Craig Chroachain, turning off at an abrupt right-angle as soon as the crossing is made. To edge its way round a bus has no more than a few inches clearance, and with a drop of fifty feet to the river below the thrill can be readily imagined.

Also on the rock face, flush with the end of the bridge, is the narrow gatehouse and entrance leading to the castle's main drive; if this is followed it will bring you to one of the most beautifully sited residences in the whole of Scotland.

Ballindalloch Castle, a trim edifice whose original portions were built about four hundred years ago, nestles in a delightful haugh close to where the Avon flows into the Spey, and the loveliness of its setting has to be seen to be believed. There is quite an interesting folk-tale as to how this site came to be chosen.

The first Grant of Ballindalloch was a son of the *Ian Mor* I have already mentioned as founding the family of Glenmoriston, and as strength rather than beauty was the virtue most desired in a residence in those days he first chose as a building site a bench on the top of Craig Chroachain, still known as the " Castle Stripe ".

When he discussed his plans with the masons the Laird thought he sensed a certain reluctance on their part, but Patrick Grant was not a man to argue with once his mind was made up, and in due course the foundations were dug and the work of building began.

At first all went well. The walls were rising at an agreeable pace until one morning the workmen assembled and made an amazing discovery. The mounting walls had completely vanished, with no trace of the missing stones to be seen.

The masons, well-grounded in local superstition, feared the worst, but when the Laird was told what had happened he dismissed all talk of supernatural agency, labelling the occurrence as the work of secret enemies, and ordering that building should go on with renewed vigour. To assist in this he greatly added to his labour force, and his orders were so energetically obeyed that by the time darkness was falling the walls were back to their former height again. When next morning dawned, however, the walls had again vanished, and the workmen were now in such a state of superstitious fear that had it not been for a comparable terror imparted by their enraged Laird they would have deserted their task there and then.

But Patrick Grant was adamant, and the work had to be begun all over again. It was only when a third morning came to disclose the same results that he expressed his views clearly.

"What enemy can be doing this?" he demanded angrily from his henchman, Ian Grant.

"The men have the belief that it is the 'good people' who do not want you to build here," was the reply.

"Good-for-nothing people!" snarled the Laird. "The work will go on and to-night I shall mount a guard who will find out the truth of this matter."

That night twenty men, armed with spear, targe and claymore, were put on watch. Stout-hearted fellows though they were, they had little liking for the task in hand. It is even doubtful if they could have brought themselves to face it had it not been that one of their number had the good sense to bring along a little keg whose contents could supply courage in the most pleasant manner possible.

"The Laird was right," cried one of the sentinels when midnight came and went without incident. "Our presence here has scared away the workmen of the night, and I think it would be safe enough now for us to lie down and get some sleep."

This was considered a good suggestion, and the guard retired to a standing of trees nearby. They were spreading their plaids before lying down when a sound made them pause. It was a distant sighing in the direction of Ben Rinnes, which grew in volume until it became a whistling, shrieking wind. With a bellowing roar it swept down upon their shelter, threatening to uproot the stout oaks over their heads, and reducing them to a state of the greatest terror.

"Would you just listen to that," cried one of the guards, his teeth chattering with fright.

The sounds he referred to were a series of loud crashes as though giant bodies of great weight were being hurled down into the stream far below. The men were so terror-stricken they dared

AT HUNTLY'S CAVE. Near legendary site of Castle Clash

JUST BEYOND THE STRATH. Dulsie Bridge is a short, scenic run from Grantown

not raise their heads. Not even when, after loud demoniac laughter, the winds departed and all was again calm. Morning dawned and their worst fears were realized. Again the whole of the previous day's work had been in vain.

When the Laird heard his watchmen's story he flew into a furious rage, accusing them of betraying him to his enemy and threatening to hang every man-jack of them. Ian Grant, however, succeeded in restraining him.

"I have fought in many a tulzie alongside those men, and I know I can trust them," said Ian. "Before passing final judgment I think it would be best if we climbed down to the waterside to test the truth of their story."

The Laird reluctantly agreed to this, and the pair descended to the banks of the Avon. Here, deep in the clear water, they could see heaps of massive and cemented stones scattered about the river bed in confusion. The Laird's brow puckered in puzzled wonder.

"There is no mark of these stones being dragged down to the water, so if this is the work of neighbouring enemies they must have enlisted the help of the devil," he said to Ian. "But I'm still determined to get to the bottom of it all. You and I shall mount guard to-night."

That day the men were encouraged to work so that when darkness fell they had a good height of wall to show for their labours. Then the Laird and Ian, fully armed and with men posted at intervals, took up their vigil. Again the night appeared to be passing peacefully enough until, close on midnight, a bellowing was heard.

"It is only the bull I had turned out into pasture," the Laird informed the men reassuringly, but their terror was such that they could not be convinced. As one man they turned and fled.

"Cowardly dogs," the Laird was growling, when all the sounds the guards described hearing on the previous night became suddenly manifest.

Then the full blast of the hurricane was upon them, taking them completely by surprise. It swept them clean over the edge of the precipice, landing them some feet down the cliff-face into the uncomfortable embrace of a holly tree. As they clung to this prickly perch they heard heavy objects rushing down over their heads and crashing into the river below. Again came

K

demoniac laughter, but followed on this occasion by a voice crying: "Build on the cow-haugh, build on the cow-haugh," as the wind faded and died away.

When morning came the Laird and his companion were found and brought up the rock face by the aid of ropes.

"What is it to be, Laird?" asked the head mason. "Do we have to start on those walls again?"

"No, Sandy," smiled the Laird. "There's nothing like the prickles of a holly bush for taking the obstinacy out of a man. We'll build, all right, but it won't be here. Muster your men and take them down to the haugh below."

It was in this way that the present site of Ballindalloch Castle came to be chosen, and who can deny that the "good people" knew what they were doing.

There have been two distinct families of Grants of Ballindalloch. The present branch are cadets of the Rothiemurchus Grants, and their progenitor was Colonel William Grant who raised one of the Independent Highland Companies incorporated into the Black Watch. He purchased the lands from the older family in 1711.

In 1806 Sir George MacPherson of Invereshie fell heir to the estates through his father's maternal uncle, General James Grant, and in 1838 he assumed the name of MacPherson-Grant. The present Laird is Sir Ewen MacPherson-Grant, ninth Baronet, and Chief of the Sliochd Gillies MacPhersons.

By the time Carron is reached the strath has temporarily relinquished its open character and become a tight glen, and from Black's Boat to this point the pace of the river's flow has increased considerably, although it is probably its swirling rush past the Rock of Tomdhu at Knockando that best earns it its title of "The Swift River". As Shaw's "History of Moray" has it:

"At the Rock of Tomdow, in this parish, the river dashes with such rapidity at right angles against the cliff, that by the violence of the collision the rafts were shattered."

The rafts referred to were those of the "floaters", log-driving from Glenmore to the sea. In face of this description a good deal must be said for the imaginative vision of a Captain Shanks of the Royal Navy, who lived at Knockando House in 1786. This gentleman declared that he had maturely considered the course of the Spey and would successfully undertake to render the river navigable for flat-bottomed boats up to forty tons all the way from the sea up to as far as Grantown-on-Spey; a distance of about sixty miles.

As there was no trade or manufacture that could possibly justify the expense of such an undertaking, this scheme was mercifully deferred to some future age when conditions might warrant its execution. I am pleased to say that time has not yet come, and I am sufficiently reactionary to hope that it never will. Still the fact that it has been considered shows that a spirit of enterprise is not lacking even in this land of hills and glens.

In Knockando churchyard are some runic stones bearing inscriptions in Scandinavian runes similar to those on the stones at Sanda Sodermanland in Sweden. They are estimated to date from the ninth or tenth century.

A pleasant half-hour's walk is all that divides Carron from Aberlour. This scrupulously clean and quaint little town is situated in the county of Banff. Its ancient name was *Skir-Drostan*, or District of St. Drostan; one more canonized member of the old Culdean Church whose existence is commemorated in place-names all over Scotland.

The name "Aberlour" is Gaelic, from *aber*, a confluence, and *laure*, a noisy, brawling stream. Some distance above the church the Lour Burn hurtles over a drop of thirty feet into a deep pool, walled by rocks twice the height of the pretty waterfall. These rocky walls magnify the sound of the tumbling waters, and the resultant reverberation (especially when a spate is on) was possibly responsible for the burn being given its descriptive name.

The town's long High Street, flanked by single-storeyed houses, many of which at the beginning of the present century were still thatched, is inordinately wide and straight. This, together with the twin rows of chubby, pollarded trees boulevarding the thoroughfare, gives the houses a miniature appearance, at once fascinating and wholly delightful.

A little less than eighty years ago Aberlour leapt into the news with a court action which only just missed becoming a *cause célèbre*. This was the Aberlour Succession Case, concerning the settlement of the will of Miss Margaret Gordon MacPherson-Grant, of Aberlour House. A very large sum of money was involved, and the press of the day reported the proceedings at great length.   Here are the main facts of the case in outline.

Miss MacPherson-Grant succeeded as heiress to her mother's brother, Alexander Grant, who had made a large fortune in the West Indies.   Her father, a MacPherson, was of much lower social standing than her mother, and her uncle had no liking either for him or his relatives; an antipathy which Miss Grant herself very much shared.

Miss MacPherson succeeded to the estate in 1854, and assumed the name of MacPherson-Grant shortly afterwards.   Ten years later, when on a visit to London, she met a Miss Charlotte Temple, daughter of the High Sheriff of Wiltshire.   To gain some inkling of what this meeting meant, let us glance at the naïve report of a local newspaper of the day.

"When the handsome, muscular Miss MacPherson-Grant met the fragile beauty of Miss Temple it was a case of love at first sight, and when Miss Grant returned to Aberlour Miss Temple came with her.   Theirs was a beautiful friendship.   So great was their mutual regard that they decided to marry each other, while at the some time vowing strict celibacy so far as the opposite sex was concerned.   Miss Grant placed a wedding-ring on Miss Temple's marriage finger and thereafter called her 'Wifie', while the latter responded by calling Miss Grant 'Jamie'."

That, then, was the set-up when Miss Temple first came to Aberlour, but after some weeks she complained of illness and wanted to go home.   Miss Grant would not hear of this at first, nursing her through the autumn and winter, but at last permitted her to go in the spring.   Within a few days of Miss Temple's departure, however, "Wifie" was receiving a telegram asking her to meet her "Jamie" in London.

This meeting took place, and the result of it was that Miss Grant made a new will, conveying her whole estate to issue of her own body, if any, and failing that, to Miss Temple and her heirs.   As Miss Grant left her solicitor's office she handed her friend a pen, saying: "I have just been making you my heir, and here is the pen I did it with—keep it! "

After that, the pair returned to Aberlour and Miss Temple settled down to her "wifely" duties.   A further will was made in 1872, naming Miss Temple's nephew as her heir, the death of her father and aunt making this adjustment necessary.   Then life for the pair went on as before—or, perhaps not quite so, for Miss Grant's bibulous habits had now increased considerably. She was drinking one and a half bottles of brandy per day, washed down by pints of draught beer out of a barrel.

On December 11th, 1875, a fire broke out at Aberlour House. Although quickly brought under control, this greatly frightened Miss Grant, her years of heavy drinking having by this time reduced her to a very bad way. She was obsessed by the idea that she had a hole in her head, and often had her hair clipped twice a day so that the servants could look for the cavity.

It was around this time that two new characters entered the story. One was a Captain Yeatman, who proposed marriage to Miss Temple and was accepted by her; the other was a Mr. Simon Keir, a London merchant who acted as factor for Miss Grant's West Indian estates. Keir was a partner in a firm whose responsibility it was to account for the returns from the Jamaican estates. Normally this was done by submission to one of Miss Grant's agents, but Mr. Keir now began forwarding these returns to Miss Grant direct, knowing full well that she was no business woman, and even refused to write a letter under any circumstances.

About a fortnight before her marriage Miss Temple wrote to Simon Keir, pointing all this out to him and requesting that future accounts be sent to Mr. Falconer, Miss Grant's solicitor in Edinburgh. Keir's response was to wait until Miss Temple had left for the south, and then himself pay a visit to Aberlour.

As a contemporary newspaper says: "What arguments he used to operate upon that diseased and decayed mind we cannot know," but the fact remains that he got her to sign a deed revoking all previous wills made by her. This was in November, 1876, and in April, 1877, she died before attaining her fiftieth year.

Miss Temple, or Mrs. Yeatman, as she now was, took immediate steps to have the deed of revocation set aside, and a jury was empanelled to decide upon the merits of her case; which was that Miss Grant had been of unsound mind when she signed the deed, and that Simon Keir had taken advantage of her mental condition to further his own ends.

The defendants in the case, apart from Keir, were some far out relatives of Miss Grant's father, named Procter. If Miss Grant's former will was revoked they were entitled, as next of kin, to succeed to an estate of over £300,000; and this despite the fact that Miss Grant had never seen or spoken to any one of them, or, perhaps, even been aware of their existence.

With such ingredients, it is easy to understand the interest of the general public in the case's outcome. As pursuer, Miss Temple's counsel had the first say in court. Possibly inspired by the ingenuousness of local newspaper reports, he went all out on a plea of "injured innocence". At the close of his address, counsel for the defence asked if the parties involved could consult together before the case was continued, and permission for this was granted. An hour later the contestants returned to the court-room and announced that they had reached a settlement, where-upon the jury was discharged.

The settlement can be summarized as follows:

(1) All allegations against Mr. Simon Keir to be withdrawn.
(2) No further attempt to impeach the deed of revocation would ever be made.
(3) The pursuer agreed to accept from the defenders the sum of £10,000 in settlement of all claims.
(4) That the remainder of the estate (amounting to more than a quarter of a million pounds) be divided equally among the next of kin.

At first sight this may seem a remarkable arrangement, but it must be remembered that although the defence had made no submission to the court they had already given to the press an indication of the course their evidence would pursue. This con-tained a multitude of promised "revelations' which the recently married Mrs. Yeatman (whom one paper described as "the in-carnation of mischief") simply could not face up to in open court.

In this way the public in general, and London society in particular, were robbed of some of the juiciest bits of scandal that had come their way in years; but, as one local paper put it: "The settlement was for the better and not for the worse, in that wealth and a fine Speyside property went to the poor, distant relations who would, no doubt, show suitable gratitude for the unexpected gift Providence had bestowed upon them."

Somewhere along the mile-long stretch of road that continues beyond the High Street one finds that Aberlour has been left behind and an unnoticed entry made to Craigellachie. Here, where the lower "Rock of Alarm" marks the end of the strath, the River Fiddich flows into the Spey, its waters spanned by a bridge every bit as difficult of negotiation as its counterpart at Ballindalloch. Again the roadway is merely a shelf cut out of the rock face, and once more it shoots off at an abrupt right angle immediately the bridge is crossed.

I once heard a motorist complain because this bridge cut down his speed from a mile per minute to a mile per hour, and I strongly sympathized with him, not because of his drop in speed, but because of his lack of ordinary perception; for this bridge at Craigellachie is really worthy of appreciation.

It is a single-arched metal span of considerable grace, and where it joins the rock are two embattled round towers, each fifty feet high. Every motorist is forced to notice these towers, while pedestrians may even find time to pause half-way to admire the magnificent view, but I wonder how many of them realize that this is a Thomas Telford bridge, which has now been in constant use for 150 years. . . . The same Telford who bridged the Menai Straits, and now lies in Westminster Abbey alongside Robert Stephenson.

In the hinterland behind the village can be seen the razor-backed peak of Ben Rinnes, 2,747 feet high, where the notorious *Seumais-nan-Tuim* had a sanctuary cave, while to the north, its pace now noticeably slackened, the Spey leaves its encompassing hills and flows through the peaceful woodlands and smiling fields of Moray on the last twenty miles of its journey to the sea.

From Kingussie to this point, the river (not the road) has covered something like eighty miles, and the long strath of Spey has at last reached its end.

CHAPTER XIII

BY THE SWIFT RIVER TO-DAY

Personal viewpoint – The strath in summer – The flowery way – A nocturnal companion – The fleeting spring – Unseasonable frosts – Spey fishing – Two kinds of shooting – Description of a hare-shoot – Local dialect – 'Characters' and their peculiarities – Celebrity parade – When 'Monty' fished the Spey – Concerning reindeer – Legend-hunting as a sport – The deer remains.

THERE is a trenchant old Scots saying which, rendered into English, tells us that "all places are all things to all men". What follows is, therefore, a strictly personal viewpoint, and it may be some clue as to how this has been arrived at if I admit to being in full agreement with Gissing's "Henry Ryecroft", when he says:

"More than half a century of existence has taught me that most of the wrong and folly which darkens earth is due to those who cannot possess their souls in quiet. Every day the world grows noisier; I for one will have no part in the increasing clamour. . . ."

In other words, I find that in Strathspey, even in this raucous age, I can achieve that measure of calm which gives life meaning; while not forgetting that this desirable attainment may be more apparent to myself than to acquaintances who imagine they know me well.

"I can't think what you find to do with yourself in a quiet place like this," said a London friend when visiting me some time ago. "Don't you find it deadly in winter?"

The answer to that question is plural, but the most complete reply is that, so far from finding myself at a loose end, and contrary to my experience when in a town, I can never find sufficient time in the twenty-four hours to do all the things I should like to.

To enlighten my friend I took him walking one day in early July, when the multitude of wild flowers in the strath were at their riotous, magnificent best. We crossed fields richly carpeted with wild pansies and scabious of a heavenly blue, passed a birch-screened bog ablaze with golden asphodel, to the foot of a towering larch-bank by the riverside where foxglove, mimulus and meadowsweet offered a supply of cut-flowers suitable for the largest vase.

Knowing my companion had the Southerner's dislike of having his attention drawn to the obvious, I refrained from commenting on the blooms around us; taking, instead, secret pleasure in the surprised wonderment nature's floral display must be causing him. It was only when we reached home that I asked him what he thought of our wild flowers.

"Flowers?" he echoed. "I didn't see any flowers; all I saw was grass."

Such imperception shocked me, until I recalled the urban belief that only grass grows in the open countryside, with flowers confined to gardens. Considered thus, it was not quite so strange. My friend only saw what he expected to see—grass!

By the same token wild animals live in zoos, so when we were out together on another day I was careful not to confuse him by pointing out a family of otters playing on the bank of a burn under a willow tree. I did, however, derive some satisfaction from his surprise and childlike delight when a family of roe-deer leapt into the roadway one afternoon, directly in the path of his car, making him pull up with a jerk. He uttered a gruff exclamation of annoyance, but I could tell by the excited light in his eyes that he was pleased; and, in a vicarious sort of way, so was I.

The wild deer population in Strathspey runs into many thousands, and unfortunate indeed is the visitor who spends any time here and departs without having seen some of them. There are occasions, though, when they can be disconcerting rather than entertaining; as a crofter acquaintance once discovered when he entered the byre for the evening milking and was sent reeling against the wall by a plump roe that was feeding in a stall alongside one of the cows.

One winter's night about five years ago I was walking back from Grantown between one and two a.m. The distance to be covered was some four miles, and the night was black with only the tree-tops showing faintly against an occasional patch of stars. I had reached the stretch of road where the Anagach Wood fringes the highway when I gradually became aware of pattering footsteps keeping pace with my own; and that at no great distance.

Thinking I was perhaps imagining things, I halted and listened. The accompanying footsteps also stopped, and all I could hear was the sighing of a light wind through the trees. When I continued on my way, however, the footfalls again became audible; closer, if anything, than before.

Shades of kelpies and the White Horse of Spey! It would have been no surprise to me just then if I had heard a seductive whinny or felt a snuffling caress on my sleeve. I went on until the wood thinned to wider-spaced trees, then stopped abruptly and crouched close to the ground.

From this position I could see the upraised head and horns of a fine buck roe silhouetted against the dim skyline. Grinning silently at the solution to the mystery I resumed an erect position and again began walking. My unusual companion kept abreast of me as far as Garrow Bridge, at which point he leapt the burn and I heard and saw no more of him.

I have since wondered what prompted that roe to walk by my side. Could it have been sheer curiosity on his part? The wind was carrying my scent away from him, and it may have been that he was as puzzled about my identity as I was about his. Or was it simply that he was lonely in the silent darkness and in search of companionship?

These are questions to which I shall never know the answer; although I do realize very fully that a townsman, or even a countryman whose mind was not entirely free from superstition, might have found that walk quite an uncomfortable experience.

Between the years 1914, when I went to the Army, and 1944, when I was invalided from the Royal Air Force, I had really seen very little of my native land, so it is scarcely surprising that one or two things in Strathspey came strange to me, especially the seasons.

Spring in the upper strath is so late and fleeting as to be almost non-existent. Until well into April (and sometimes May) the deciduous trees are quite black and leafless, then in a brief matter of days birch, rowan, gean and alder are cloaked in vernal green, and the little clans of the woodland are making a reborn world gay with their song. Burns, swollen to the size of turbulent rivers by the melting of upland snows roar hoarse threats and consume all things that try to obstruct their course until, practically overnight, the growl dies in their throats leaving nothing but a babbling sweetness to mingle with the bird-song.

Summers are short, and in a normal year really hot weather comes only in the months of July and August. There are, of course, exceptions to this rule. In 1947, for instance, the sun blazed forth strongly towards the middle of June *and* kept that way on each successive day right up to the third week in September, while in 1955 the summer was even longer and more perfect still.

To live in Strathspey under such conditions is to know a foretaste of paradise. No matter how hot the sun (and it can climb into the "eighties") the air retains a wine-like quality; akin to what I have experienced on an African or Canadian morning, but equalled nowhere else in Britain.

Unfortunately, such a long spell of perfect weather cannot be regarded as the norm, and even though the measured annual rainfall is far below the average for the remainder of Britain, we still have to remember that this is mountain country, with all the freak weather that can imply.

In 1952, after the nearest approach to a Lowland spring I have ever known here, the gardens were very well forward, showing every promise of a record year for flowers, fruit and vegetables. Alas, on the night of June 23rd there came 10 degrees of frost, and when morning dawned the fecund gardens of the day before had been reduced to patches of black and utter ruin.

Worse still was an August night of 1945. On this occasion the temperature dropped in twelve hours from 80 degrees in the shade to 16 degrees of frost, and then, within the next half-day, climbed back to the eighties again. The devastation this caused was unbelievable. Ripening golden corn was turned a sickly grey, and the green acres of root crops were blackened as though by an all-devouring fire.

Needless to say, frosts of this kind also are exceptional; but the wise gardener is he who plants late, so that crops like potatoes do not show through the ground until June is gone.

Compared with other Scottish rivers, such as the Tay, the fishing season on the Spey starts late and finishes early; that is,

angling begins well on in February and closes towards the beginning of October. Between these dates, however, the Angling
Associations, not to mention the parties who rent private
water, can do battle for eight months in the year with the most
sporting fish in these islands; the lean-headed, shark-like Spey
salmon.

In this Age of the Common Man there is a sensitive tendency
to regard angling for salmon as a relaxation of the idle rich, a
"snob" pastime, but here in Strathspey it does not work out
quite that way.

You can, of course, if you are terribly wealthy, pay £90 per
week for a five mile beat of the river, but for residents in the
Grantown area a full-membership, salmon-fishing ticket from the
Strathspey Angling Association costs only One Guinea per
annum, with rights to fish thirteen miles of banks where
the Spey harbours some of its most sporting and productive
pools.

With charges at this reasonable rate it can be seen how
ridiculous are petty aspersions about a "snob" pastime. The
great majority of men who fish the Spey are neither idle nor
rich. They are the labourers in the field, hard-working shop-
keepers and professional men, in fact, everyone who has the good
fortune to live in this locality.

Add to this that *all* burns and many lochs in Strathspey are
completely free to anyone who wants to indulge in angling, and
it will soon be realized what a Mecca for fishermen we have here.
The majority of local wiseacres will tell you that "the worm is
the thing" when going after burn trout, but I, personally, have
long proved that equally excellent results can be obtained with
the right sort of fly.

A year or two ago, when rationing was stringent, I had a friend
drop in unexpectedly and felt it incumbent upon me to offer
him lunch. As, however, he happened to be my third lunch-
time visitor that week there was simply nothing in the larder
to give him. I solved the problem by picking up two fishing-
rods, presenting him with one and retaining the other
myself.

"Come on," I invited. "The burn is right by the house, and
I'm afraid I'll have to ask you to fish for your lunch."

We were gone only ten minutes. When we returned we had

2¼ lbs. of fish; three burn trout of ½ lb. each, and one brown trout of ¾ lb. One minute, no lunch; twenty minutes later—fish and chips! It was as easy as that. Who now can deny that there is some advantage in living in a Highland glen?

I have also heard shooting condemned by the neo-democrat as a reprehensible pastime and evidence of shameless wealth. But, here again, this need not necessarily be right so far as Strathspey is concerned.

We do, of course, have grouse drives in August, or pheasant shoots in November, when wealthy sportsmen bring unwonted life to our hills and woods, and we see no reason why we should not extend to them the same warm welcome we bestow upon less celebrated visitors. After all, they pay our school children on holiday £1 per day for beating, and this solves the problems of many a harassed parent when it comes to clothing their offspring throughout the year.

I notice that the really stylish shoots nowadays no longer rely upon ponies and hampers to provide them with the means of sustenance through a hot and tiring day. They have their own chuck-wagon, complete with electric cooker, deep-freeze, and all the other gadgets necessary for the supply of a freshly-cooked meal, washed down by a suitably chilled wine.

In fact, the old *Punch* cartoon depicting a bibulous colonel confiding in a fellow officer that his day's bag had been "a magnum of Chateau Yquem, a Veuve Clicquot, and two Chambertins", would now be sadly out-of-date. The colonel's type no longer has need to forage as of old, and still less for boasting over spoils so easily obtained.

So far I have never been out on a shoot of this kind, and cannot, therefore, pass an opinion on its entertainment value, but I am completely without reservations when it comes to declaring the enjoyment I derive from shoots of another kind. These take place much later in the year, and every gun carries such refreshment as he may require on his own person.

Permission for these shoots is most thoughtfully provided by the present owner of Castle Grant, the Countess of Seafield, and the arranging of them is very capably carried out by headkeeper Coupland. They are held in the depths of winter, from December to February, in all kinds of weather, after all sorts of game—and the fun is tremendous! Doctors, parsons, local government officials, crofters, shop-keepers, errand-boys, in fact "a' bodies", are present, armed with every sort of gun from Crimean War days up to the latest ejector pump-guns. Some shoots are all-in affairs, when the beaters, blazing away merrily as they go, drive everything before them so that the day's bag, divided equally all round, consists of just about everything from black game, woodcock, pheasant, capercaillie, rabbits and hares to roe-deer and, sometimes (yes; it must be admitted), less conventional game. On one never-to-be-forgotten occasion our poaching ginger tom-cat was mistaken by a beater for a steal-away fox and, alas, was promptly killed.

A few days before writing these lines I was out on a hare-shoot over the braes separating the parish of Cromdale from Dava Moor. The view from up there is magnificent at this time of the year, every peak and detail of the snow-shrouded Cairngorms being clearly visible from surroundings themselves as wild as one can possibly imagine.

Patches of the winter's snow were still lying in drifts five feet deep in places, and the going, whether on hill or moss, was atrocious. On parts of the hill the heather was almost waist high and the moss was just one large boggy ooze of water where one often sank to the knees.

But no one heeded the going; or the icy wind that blew chill rain straight from the snow-covered mountains. The hares were running, and as there was not enough of us for a drive we walked up on them, picking up and carrying as we killed.

After the first few shots the scene was indescribable. I never realized before that there could be so many of these creatures in the world; certainly not within such a restricted area. There were hundreds of them, and what a spectacle they made crossing and criss-crossing the hill-side, their snow-white coats showing up in startling fashion against the blackish, dull brown of the heather.

We ploughed our way through six miles of bog, after having covered four miles of hill and heather to get to our starting point. Our bag was 112 hares, and I do not mind admitting that I was tired by the time we got back to where we had left the cars. What, then, must the man on my right have felt like? He was thin and frail-looking, over seventy, and had been compulsorily retired from work some years before on account of a heart condition. He was carrying seventeen hares, averaging 7 lbs. each, yet he assured me he was "feeling fine" and that his hundred-weight load was nothing to talk about.

These winter shoots bring much welcome replenishment to the larder, and many a local lady has benefited by a handsome stole from the pelt her husband obtained when out on a fox-shoot.

The summer, with its hill-climbs, loch-bathing and fishing, can be very pleasant, but I still think I like the winter best. In the season of short days and long nights we are a community entirely unto ourselves, and on a surprising number of days the sun shines out of a cloudless sky, even when the temperature has dropped below zero. When this happens, with mountains looking like white cardboard cut-outs against a backdrop of vivid blue, the similarity of the surroundings to the Swiss Alps is so striking that it is difficult to remember that this is really Britain.

The 1951 census showed that there were only two inhabitants in my village who still had the Gaelic, but there are other parts of Strathspey where users of the "Language of Eden" would make a slightly better showing. Unlike the softer-spoken North-west Highlands, displacement of the native tongue in Strathspey came from the Laigh of Moray. This has resulted in a dialect at once pithy and more reminiscent of Buchan than the Highlands. Through it all, though, legacies of the Gaelic still remain.

When I was a boy the change-over to English had not travelled quite so far as it has done to-day. At that time the Highlander's chief difficulty lay in the matter of gender, so that he invariably said "she" when what he really meant was "he" or "it". In Strathspey at the present day that obstacle is surmounted, but tenses, together with the singular and plural, are apparently still in need of adjustment. Here is a scrap of conversation over-heard between two women in a bus last summer. It should offer an illustration.

"Hoo's the peas the year?"

"That blackies has been at them."

"I thought I heard a shoot your way; what was in it?"

"I got the keeper to come and shot that birds; that's what was in it."

When first encountered this dialect sounds strange to the ear, but it is surprising how soon one can get used to it.

Another distinctive feature of our local population is the number of "characters" it has always contained, and if the Eppie Laings and Mad Chalmers of a former day were to revisit us they would find counterparts to welcome them.

One poor lad from Grantown, who was put off balance by an injury during the First World War, blends a great love for the natural scene with a most disconcerting habit of roosting in trees. One day I was walking through a wood during a severe frost with the thermometer reading minus several degrees. There was a great stillness everywhere and I should have said that I was the only person abroad for miles around. Then I became aware of a strange crooning; eerie and difficult to locate, until I realized it was coming from somewhere above my head. I looked up. There, perched high on a pine branch and looking for all the world like a monstrous, bedraggled crow, was the "harmless one". He was swaying slightly, staring out into nothingness and singing softly to himself, apparently quite happy and without a care in the world.

It is also no unusual sight in the depths of winter to come upon this same man lying sprawled out on a snow-bank, fast asleep and with his face upturned to the sun.

A character of a more amusing type occasionally comes in to Grantown from an outlying hill croft. He loves a "news" (gossip) and invariably buttonholes me when we meet in the street, possibly because I am one of the few who can find time to listen to him and not think him boring. From my first talk with this old fellow I gathered that his *bête noir* was "that man" who had started a war in which seven of his relatives, "all fine lads", were killed.

My first assumption was that Hitler was the "that man" referred to, then from other remarks I began to wonder if it might not really be the Kaiser, or even Paul Kruger, who was being alluded to. It was only after I became better acquainted with my friend from the hills, and learned most of his own personal history, that I discovered how wide of the mark I had been.

This crofter is over seventy, and was brought up from child-hood by a great-aunt who died at the turn of the century in her

IN CASTLE GRANT. Waitt's portrait of Champion Alistair Mor

CLERIC AND GENEALOGIST. Waitt's portrait of the Rev. James Chapman

97th year. It was *her* father's seven brothers who had been killed, and the "that man" my quaint friend is still reviling was *Napoleon!*

That, I realize, may sound fantastic, but it is true, and the unforgiving dislike of my long-memoried friend is very real.

Hotels throughout Strathspey are very comfortable, and not only cater well for visitors but provide an excellent objective for those who, like myself, prefer to have a goal at the end of a walk rather than simply amble along for exercise's sake.

One morning I looked in at a Grantown hotel after a four mile stroll and had an encounter which sticks in my memory. It was about six weeks before "D" Day and I had only recently been invalided from the Service. While enjoying my refreshment in the hotel lounge I was accosted by a somewhat brainless type of Army officer, who was apparently anxious to impress a "civvy" like myself with the extent of his military knowledge. According to him, a landing was due to take place on the Continent within the next forty-eight hours, and he was evidently offended when I stopped him from going into details by suggesting that he keep a guard on his tongue.

This officer's indiscretion worried me throughout the whole of my walk home. How could any element of surprise be attained if that sort of idiot was allowed to roam at large? I was still thinking thus, and had just reached the Boat House close to where I was living, when two dark saloon cars drew up a few yards ahead of me. From one stepped out a uniformed batman carrying a luncheon-basket, and from the other alighted General Montgomery with his Chief of Staff, General De Guingand. . . . How empty my fears of a moment before looked just then, and I regretted that the line-shooter had not elected to walk back with me.

"Monty" had been inspecting some units at Invergordon, and had stopped for a few hours fishing at the invitation of my neighbour, Major Edwards, who, like myself, was renting a farm-house at the time. I am pleased to say our Commander-in-Chief had an hour or two of reasonable sport, even though the fish he got into, a big fellow, "broke" him after a twenty-minute battle. His Chief-of-Staff was more fortunate in that he had something to show for his labours; a 2 lb. sea-trout. Six weeks after this came the Normandy landings.

L

Mention of this reminds me that it is not only Napoleon-hating hill-crofters one is likely to see in Grantown's High Street. Celebrity-hunting is not a local pastime, possibly because Spey-siders are too well catered for in this respect. Here it is possible for notables of every grade, from royalty to the most publicized stage or screen star of the day, to go about a morning's shopping with all the anonymity of citizens in less exalted spheres. A consideration for which royalty, at least, must be grateful.

A recent topic of more than local interest has been the arrival at Rothiemurchus of two small herds of reindeer. There was a number of deaths among the first batch to reach here, but the second lot, wood-reindeer in this instance, appear to be doing well.

So far I have indicated quite a number of ways of employing one's time in Strathspey; walking, climbing, fishing, shooting, bathing, gardening, etc.; but I really must not overlook one other recreation, most important so far as my tastes are concerned. I am referring to legend-hunting, which incidentally differs greatly from legend-collecting.

The legend-collector need only be the veriest bookworm, reticent, unsociable, and never to be found too far from the reading-room of a Reference Library. The legend-hunter, on the other hand, is a very different kind of being. He shows a willing-ness to face the hill in all weathers, is capable of friendly con-versation, and is the possessor of a retentive memory. But the greatest difference between the two probably lies in the fact that the " collector " does not care whence his legends come, while the " hunter " concentrates his efforts in unearthing old tales that have yet to see print.

Sometimes the results are most satisfying, at others madden-ingly elusive and demanding high qualities of perseverance. There are occasions when the tales come in distorted fragments, only obtained by tramping miles over hill and moor to outlying croft or shepherd's bothy; or, such is the luck of the game, can be picked up whole and complete simply by visiting the warmth and comfort of a cosy bar parlour.

Recent additions to the attractions of Strathspey as a holiday resort include ski-ing, pony-trekking, and angling courses under expert tuition, all introduced by the Scottish Council for Physical Recreation. This is having the gratifying effect of extending by some two months "the season" for the local hoteliers, as well as providing relaxation to thousands of visitors, who could not find a comparable holiday anywhere else in Britain.

In closing this account of Strathspey, I hope I have said enough to indicate that its inhabitants are still proving worthy of their heritage, that the deer remains on the hill, and that a friendly welcome can yet be expected by those who come to see for themselves this lovely land where the swift river runs.

NOTE ON THE GRANTS OF STRATHSPEY

Three distinct claims are made when it comes to deducing the origin of Clan Grant; one Scandinavian, one Celtic, and one Norman.

The Norman claim was the last to be put forward, and this at a period during the Victorian era when it was fashionable for anyone with any pretensions to blue blood to claim descent either from the Conqueror himself or one of his followers, who, incidentally, included quite a number of expatriate Scots mercenaries. A Bruce and a Comyn, for instance, came over with William, but these names were known in the Highlands and Islands for at least five hundred years before that and there is some evidence that there were Grants in Ireland prior to the Norman invasion.

So far as the Grants are concerned, a Norman genealogy is no more supported by conclusive evidence than are the counter claims. The probability is that their lineage was ancient and noble long before the Norman Conqueror was ever heard of.

The case for a Scandinavian descent is set forth in *An Account of the Rise and Offspring of the Name of Grant*, by the Rev. James Chapman, minister of the Kirk of Cromdale from 1702 to 1737. This is a truly remarkable document. In its 40 octavo pages it traces the Grant lineage back through two Norse kings to Woden, the Viking demi-god, using his thrice-royal ancestry as an explanation for the *"Three antique crowns, or"* noted in the Grant armorial bearings as far back as 1325.

The significance of these "Three antique crowns" is disregarded by the strictly orthodox historian, yet they are unique in heraldry and no explanation, other than the Rev. Mr. Chapman's, has ever been put forward for their adoption.

The principal champion for the Anglo-Norman theory was the late Sir William Fraser, LL.D., whose monumental work, *the Chiefs of Grant*, was published privately in 1883. This history, in three imposing volumes, is chiefly valuable for its transcriptions of letters and ancient charters from the Grant muniment chest. It is also a good reference-source for documented dates, but when the learned doctor allows himself to indulge in speculation its usefulness ends.

First of all, he quotes the name 'le Grant' from fourteenth

century documents as a proof that the early Grants must have been Anglo-Normans; overlooking the fact that the Scottish Court of the period was Normanized, and this form of nomenclature fashionable. To persist in such an argument would make Sir John le Graham and Sir Walter de Ogilvie, two of the most ancient Celtic names in Scotland, also of Norman origin.

He then goes on to point out that the Grantemesnil family, who are noted in the Domesday Book as having come to England with the Conqueror, had as their motto: "*Tenons ferme*", and remarks on the likeness of this to the Grant motto: "Stand Fast". He could, with equal profit, have gone a step further and shown that the Grantemesnil motto is practically identical with that of the Leslies: "Grip Fast".

Dr. Black, in his *Surnames of Scotland*, not only follows Fraser without question in this respect but goes one better when he states categorically that the French motto *means* "Stand Fast".

One could go on for pages showing how completely lacking in proof are all the claims Sir William Fraser puts forward for an Anglo-Norman descent, but we will assume that enough has already been said and examine those favouring a Celtic origin.

Some protagonists of this descent say that the Grants had as ancestor Donald Mor MacGregor, who lived in Stratherrick in the twelfth century. Others assume that the name 'Grant' comes from *Sliabh Griantias*, Plain of the Sun, a district in Strathspey now known as Dava Moor. A final deduction is that Grant comes from a Gaelic word meaning 'grey' or 'hoary'; although the authorities putting this forward never tell us exactly what the word is. There is a possibility that I may be able to offer some enlightenment in this respect.

My interest in Highland clans goes back over a considerable number of years, and as a very young man I had the habit of jotting down all sorts of stray matter concerning them. Unfortunately, having no thought that the day might come when I should want to share my gleanings with others, I very often neglected to note the sources of the data I was recording. Where the information was traditional, this did not matter much, but where strictly historical material was concerned it was most tantalizing when, in later years, I wanted to make use of some of my notes and could not do so for lack of a quotable authority.

The following interesting item, which I set great store by, falls into this category. I picked it up while serving with the Ulster Division in France during the First World War, taking it from a North Irish newspaper, the name and date of which, in my callow, careless manner, I neglected to record. Here it is:

"The Grahans, whose name means 'hoary', were Gallgaels whose lands ran down from the Glynns of Antrim to the shores of Loch Grahan. 'Grahan of the Glynns' is noted arriving in Tyrconnell in the tenth century, and we are told that he was a powerful chieftain and a great sage. In the thirteenth century the name was noted in Scotland as 'Graand' or 'Grant', and in Ulster it was later Englished into 'Strahan'. Other spellings of the name were 'Straughan' or 'Strang', and Loch Grahan became Strangford Loch, as it still remains."

This reference to the name 'Strahan' (with variations in spelling such as 'Strachan' and 'Strachon') I consider of the greatest significance because it is noted in the Grant territory of Strathspey right through the centuries; even here in my own parish of Cromdale, as the following extract from the seventeenth century Records of the Inverness Burgh Court clearly shows:

"*That day (15th September)—Grant in Cromdail, for the bluid latting of Georg Strachon, and sticking him with ane knife, breaking the kingis pace, trubling the toun and mercat, is convicted.*"

The Records then go on to show that George Strachon was also convicted for retaliating with "ane durck"; although Grant received the larger fine.

Another indication of Celtic descent is that the Grants have always been closely allied with the MacGregors and are accepted as a branch of the ancient, and highly conservative, *Siol Alpine*. This is made up of eight clans; the Grants, MacAlpines, MacAulays, MacGregors, MacKinnons, MacNabs, MacPhees and MacQuarries; all of whom claim descent from Alpin, King of Scots.

Skene, in his *Highlanders of Scotland*, dismisses this claim of royal descent, relying upon the Gaelic MS. of 1450 which makes no mention of it and places the Clan Alpine among the rebellious Moray tribes transplanted by Malcolm IV. This, however, contains one glaring discrepancy. The reference *could* apply to the MacAlpines, but not to the *Siol Alpine* as a whole, because clans like the MacAulays, MacKinnons and MacQuarries were holding lands in the Western Isles around this time and Malcolm could not have placed them there; these territories, ruled by the Regulus of the Isles, being outwith his kingdom.

A feature of *Siol Alpine* was their remarkable regard for kinship. Although their clan territories were scattered far apart throughout the Highlands and Isles the closest bonds of friendship always existed between them, and all, including the Grants, wear as their distinguishing clan badge, the pine.

When the MacGregors were proscribed and hunted throughout the length and breadth of the land at the beginning of the seventeenth century we find the Laird of Grant giving them sanctuary; braving the king's wrath to do so, and ultimately paying a fine of 16,000 merks rather than prove unfaithful to men of his kin.

The circumstance that really makes descent from Alpin suspect is the fact that he was of Brythonic (Cymric) origin, from the ancient Kingdom of Strathclyde, while *Siol Alpine* names like MacQuarrie (Son of the Noble One) and MacAulay (Son of Olaf) are Gallgael. It could be, though, that the marriage of a common ancestor with a daughter of the Brythonic king was the reason for this claim.

All this may be no more than matter for conjecture, yet it cannot be entirely ignored. There is also another aid towards discovering racial origin which historians seldom pay any attention to. This is the science of ethnology, and there are those among us, myself included, who most shamelessly insist that cephalic measurements, colouring and other physical characteristics are often more faithful guides in this respect than all the musty documents that were ever penned. Here is an instance to show how fatal it is to depend entirely upon written evidence when assessing a man's origin.

In 1923 I met a man in Vera Cruz, Mexico, whose every feature proclaimed him a Celt, yet who answered to a Spanish name. He achieved great national prominence, was assassinated within a year of my meeting with him, and has since been given a genealogy carefully blended between the Aztec and aristocratic Castilian that is in all ways fitting for a Mexican hero. . . . The truth is he was an Irishman, and his real name was O'Brien.

With the Grants there are three outstanding or predominant types of physiognomy, suggesting three different racial origins—Gallgael (a fusion of Pictish Irish with Norse), Norse, and Cymric. The present Chief of the Clan, Lord Strathspey, has the Gallgael type of features, Nina, Countess of Seafield, the Norse, while the very fine portrait of Grant of Lurg at Doune House is a good representative of the Cymric.

It is, therefore, not to official documents but towards these strongly preserved clan features we must turn for a possible explanation of the " *Three antique crowns, or* ". Alpin *could* have been the source of one of these crowns, Ulster and Norse kings that of the other two.

One tradition has it the Clan Chiaran and Clan Alanach Grants were the first to settle in Strathspey, taking up residence at Achnarrow and Dunan and later moving across the river to Delachapple and Auchernach—all these places being in the present parish of

Cromdale—but this is more than doubtful. Lachlan Shaw, in his *History of Moray*, says of them:

"The names of their ancient or old seats in Stratherrick (as Gartmore, Gartinbeg, Dillachapple, etc.) were given to their new seats in Strathspey. But at what time they came into Strathspey (surely not all at one time) I pretend not to determine."

Sir William Fraser scornfully dismisses this similarity of place-names, saying they are usual throughout Scotland to describe local features and lacking any other significance. I cannot agree with him there, because nowhere else in Scotland, other than Stratherrick and Strathspey, are *all* these places to be found, cheek by jowl, within one restricted area.

The first recorded home of the Grants was Stratherrick, Inverness-shire, and all speculation as to their origin apart, we have the backing of fully documented history to tell us when the first of the name entered Strathspey. This was when the monks of Inverallan granted a charter of their lands to John le Grant (1316), and these are still retained by his descendants more than six hundred years later.

The first historic mention of the Grants as a 'clan' is in 1527. Ten years after this an instrument relating to parishioners in Duthil contains many different Celtic clan names, but when a further twenty years have elapsed another document shows that about 65 per cent of people in the parish were by then named 'Grant'.

This is generally presumed to indicate that tenants of Grant holdings were forced to take the clan name, and John MacConnachie (MacDonnachaidh—Son of Duncan) of Gartinbeg is quoted as an example of this. In 1537 he is designated "MacConquhy", but in 1581 his son is described as Duncan Grant. All this really proves is that surnames, as opposed to patronymics, were not in common use in Strathspey at this time, any more than they were in other parts of the Highlands two centuries later, and the real fact of the matter is that the full name of the John MacConquhy mentioned was actually John MacConnachie Grant, or John, Son of Duncan Grant. This is established by yet another document in which he is so described.

Some tenants did, of course, change their name to 'Grant', but not nearly so many as has been supposed. Nor did the clan occupy the whole of Strathspey in one fell swoop. This took time, shrewd purchase, judicious marriage, much sagacity and, occasionally, use of force.

What the Grants took, they held. But it can be said in their favour that the fruits of their conquest were always improved and never despoiled.

BIOGRAPHICAL NOTE ON THE CHIEFS OF GRANT

1. GREGOR DE GRANT

Date of chiefship is controversial. Credited with being Sheriff Principal of Inverness during reign of Alexander II. Had four sons, Laurence, Robert, Lucas and Alan.

2. SIR LAURENCE DE GRANT

Was Chief in 1258. Mentioned in "Rhymer's Federa" as friend and kinsman of Walter Bisset. Held lands in Stratherrick. Had two sons, John and Rudolph.

3. SIR JOHN GRANT

A great patriot who nobly supported Sir William Wallace in the fight for Scottish Independence. Imprisoned by Edward I of England in 1296, and liberated on bail in the following year. Succeeded by his eldest son:

4. SIR JOHN GRANT

Commanded right wing of Scots Army at Battle of Halidonhill, 19th July, 1338. Received order of knighthood from David II. Was one of the Ambassadors Extraordinary appointed to the Court of France. The first of his name to receive lands in Strathspey, and probably the first to be designated "of Freuchie". Left one son, Robert, and a daughter, Agnes.

5. SIR ROBERT GRANT

Much in favour with King Robert II. His prominence is underlined by the share he received of the 40,000 francs sent by the King of France to be divided among the nobility and principal gentry of Scotland. Died during the reign of King Robert III. Was greatly esteemed for his conduct and fortitude. Succeeded by his son:

6. MALCOLM GRANT

One of the gentlemen of rank and distinction mentioned as member of a convention for settling a dispute between Thomas Dunbar, Earl of Moray, and Alexander, Lord of the Isles. Died towards the close of the fourteenth century. Succeeded by his son:

7. SIR PATRICK GRANT

Mentioned in a charter in the Grant Archives as "Patricius de Grant, Dominus de Stratherrick" in which he gives his daughter and her husband a life rent of certain lands in Strathspey. Twice married; his second wife being a daughter of MacLean of Duart who was killed at the Battle of Harlaw, 1411. She supplied him with an heir. Sir Patrick was a man of great activity and prudence who considerably increased the fortunes of his family.

8. SIR JOHN GRANT

Sheriff Principal of Inverness. A musket of his, bearing the "three antique crowns," of the family arms and dated 1434, is still in the Grant possession. Greatly furthered the friendship between his mother's people, the MacLeans of Duart, and the Grants. Married Matilda (Bigla) Cumming. Had three sons, the eldest of whom was Duncan.

9. SIR DUNCAN GRANT

Dr. Forsyth begins his list of Chiefs with this Sir Duncan, and Sir William Fraser claims he was the first of the exclusively "Freuchie" Grants. The latter also asserts that his mother, Matilda, was not a Cumming, but a descendant of Malise, Ancient Celtic Earl of Strathearn. He says that from the date of Sir Duncan's accession (1434) down to the present day the long chain in the Grant ancestry is clearly attested by authentic evidence. Sir Duncan had twin sons, the second of whom was progenitor of the Grants of Ballindalloch. He outlived both. When he died in 1475 he was succeeded by his grandson:

10. JOHN GRANT

During the reign of this Chief we first see the Grants being officially recorded as a "clan". He married Margaret Ogilvie, daughter of Sir James Oglivie of Deskford, the first of several marriage contracts between the two families. He died in 1482, and was succeeded by his son:

11. JOHN GRANT

Called *Iain-nan-Bard Roy*, "John, the Red Poet". He died about 1528 and was succeeded by the eldest of his three sons:

12. JAMES GRANT

Known as *Seumais-nan-Creach*, "James of the Forays". Held the chiefship in very troublous times and, as his by-name implies, was equal to all the warlike deeds he was called upon to perform. Much esteemed by King James V, who used his services to keep the other clans in order. He died in 1553.[1]

13. JOHN GRANT

Son of the warlike James, he was known as *Iain Baold*, or "John the Gentle" (q.v. 'Simple'). Was twice married. By his second wife, Mary, daughter of Colin, Earl of Argyle, had two sons and two daughters. The second son, Patrick, was ancestor of the Grants of Rothiemurchus. This John was everything a patriarchal Chief should be, and was much loved by his clansmen. He outlived his eldest son, and when he died (1585) he was succeeded by his grandson:

14. JOHN GRANT OF FREUCHIE

Is remarkable in that he was peculiarly known as "of Freuchie". Was Chief of the Grants at the time of the Battle of Glenlivet, when the defection of the Grants from the left wing of Argyle's army (previously arranged with Huntly) contributed greatly to the young Campbell Chief's defeat. He purchased the Lordship of Abernethy from the Earl of Moray for 22,000 merks, and so greatly extended the Grant possessions that he was considered the richest and most extensive landowner in the North. He also settled his brothers in fine estates—Patrick, in Wester Elchies, James in Ardnilly, and Robert in Lurg. King James VI and his Queen were present at his wedding to Lillias Mary, daughter of the Earl of Athole. She bore him one son and four daughters. He had a natural son, Duncan, who founded the house of Clury.

15. SIR JOHN GRANT

Became Chief in 1622. Entering into wide possessions, he greatly impaired the family fortunes by the magnificent and profligate manner of his living. He sold the estate of Lethen, which his father had acquired, to Alexander Brodie. He married May Ogilvie, daughter of Walter, Lord Ogilvie, of Deskford, and by her had eight sons and three daughters. One daughter, Mary, who married Lord Lewis Gordon in 1644, lived to a great age. She died in 1712.

16. JAMES GRANT

Succeeded his father in 1637. Although a Covenanter, he was also a fervid Royalist and much respected by the King. He married May, daughter of James, Earl of Moray. The marriage was performed by the Rev. Gilbert Marshall, Minister of Cromdale, who

[1] Sir William Fraser disputes this, saying he died in 1533, and that his son held the chiefship for fifty-two years.

was later disciplined for the action by the Synod of Moray. Lady Grant lived and died a Roman Catholic. Her funeral at Duthil, 30th December, 1662, was the last occasion on which the crucifix was carried in Strathspey. Sir James died in Edinburgh, where he had gone to defend Alan Grant of Tulloch against a charge of man-slaughter. "He was successful in preserving the life of his friend, but could not prolong his own," is how Dr. Forsyth puts it. He was buried in the Abbey Church of Holyrood in 1663.

17. LUDOVICK GRANT

Was a minor when he succeeded in 1663. A chief in the true Celtic tradition, his bearing was so regal that James, Duke of York inadvertently addressed him as "Your Highland Majesty." He was twice married; first to Janet Brodie, by whom he had four sons and four daughters, and secondly to Jean, daughter of Sir John Houston, by whom he had no children. Guiding his people through difficult times he was in every way an outstanding Chief. Like his father, he died in Edinburgh and was buried in the Abbey Church of Holyrood in 1716.

18. ALEXANDER GRANT

Liked the military life, and as a character could not be termed outstanding. His youngest sister, Margaret, married the notorious Simon, Lord Lovat, in 1716. In Strathspey the wedding was cele-brated in traditional Highland fashion, with long days of feasting and dancing, and bonfires blazing on every height. A close friend of John, Duke of Argyle, Alexander commanded a Regiment of Foot and rose to the rank of Brigadier-General. He also died in Edinburgh, and was the third successive Laird of Grant to be buried in the Abbey Church of Holyrood (1719). Unmarried, he was succeeded by his brother:

19. JAMES GRANT

Second son of Ludovick, he became Chief in 1719. In 1702 he married Ann, daugher and heiress of Sir Humphrey Colquhoun. Was strongly anti-Jacobite, and when Prince Charles Edward wrote to him making urgent appeal for support he returned the letter unopened. This, despite the fact that some of the ablest of his kinsmen, such as the Grants of Glenmoriston and Grant of Burn-side, turned out and fought valiantly for the Prince. By his wife, Ann, he had five sons and five daughters. He preferred the life of country gentleman, and was responsible for much valuable afforesta-tion in Strathspey, being the first to introduce larch into this area. He was succeeded by his second son:

20. SIR LUDOVICK GRANT

Succeeded in 1747. Married Lady Margaret Ogilvie, daughter of James, Fifth Earl of Findlater and Seafield, and by this marriage, the third solemnized between a Grant Chief and an Ogilvie, the Ogilvie estates finally came to the Grant family. Sir Ludovick was an able Laird, a progressive agriculturalist, and a great improver and benefactor of his lands. He projected the Strathspey Academy at Cromdale, but owing to the unfortunate fight between rival clan factions there this never came into being. It was this same incident that was responsible for him founding the town of Grantown. He was a Member of Parliament for twenty years, representing the County of Moray, and by his wife had one son and eleven daughters. In his twenty-six years as Chief he did much to improve the lot of his clansfolk, and was fortunate in having a son more than willing to continue his good work. He died at Castle Grant, Cromdale, in 1773, and was interred in the family burial place at Duthil.

21. SIR JAMES GRANT

Was known as "The Good Sir James". Renowned for his spirit of justice and benevolence, he lived in close touch with his people and took great interest in their welfare. Lachlan Shaw, who knew him well, tells us: "He was affable and courteous in his deportment, distinguished for his charity, hospitality and beneficence. He was dignified without pride . . . and courteous without deceit." He continued with many of the schemes his father inaugurated and was the real founder of Grantown, although it was his father who first planned the town. He made roads, built bridges, erected a town house and jail, and fostered industries such as weaving, dyeing, brewing, etc. He also gave special attention to education, erecting a school in Grantown to take the place of the academy originally proposed for Cromdale. He raised a regiment of Fencibles and the 97th Regiment of the Line, and at different times represented the counties of Moray and Banff in Parliament. Married to Jane Duff, daughter of the 1st Earl of Fife, he had seven sons and six daughters. He died in 1811 and was succeeded by his son:

22. LEWIS ALEXANDER OGILVIE-GRANT

Was educated at St. Paul's, Westminster, and Edinburgh University. Showed every promise of having a brilliant career at the bar. Was M.P. for Elgin and Nairn, and his speech in the Warren Hastings debates (1790) brought forth the commendation of Fox. A year later his mind gave way and he was forced to live in retirement at Cullen House and Grant Lodge, Elgin. His uncle, the 4th Earl of Seafield, dying in 1811, he succeeded to this peerage and took the name 'Ogilvie-Grant'. He died in 1840 and was succeeded by his brother:

23. FRANCIS WILLIAM OGILVIE-GRANT
6th Earl of Seafield

Was the second son of the Good Sir James. He was generally known as Colonel Grant. He entered the Army at the age of fifteen, and a year later was Lieut.-Colonel of the Colonsay Fencibles, with permanent rank in the Army. At the age of seventeen he took his regiment overseas. After retiring from the Army he was a Member of Parliament for 38 years. Celebrated for his activities in afforestation, he planted 31,686,482 trees; pine, larch and hardwood. Married Mary Anne, daughter of John Charles Dun, of Higham House, and by her had six sons and a daughter. Suffered a double bereavement when his wife and eldest son died within a few days of each other the son being drowned in the Spey at Cromdale when hastening home for his mother's funeral. This son, Francis William, was twenty-six years old, and a young man of great promise. Colonel Grant was succeeded by his second son:

24. JOHN CHARLES OGILVIE-GRANT
7th Earl of Seafield

Was created a Peer of the United Kingdom under the title, Baron Strathspey. He was born 1814, and entered the Navy as a Midshipman at the age of fourteen. He was serving under Sir John Franklin when he retired on the death of his elder brother. We are told he was "loyal to the principles of his house and the history of his clan". He shared his father's love for afforestation and some of the trees planted by him were blown down in the great gale of 31st of January, 1953. He married the Hon. Caroline Stewart, youngest daughter of the 11th Lord Blantyre. He died at Cullen House in 1881, and was succeeded by his only child:

25. IAN CHARLES OGILVIE-GRANT
8th Earl of Seafield, Viscount Reidhaven, Baron Ogilvie of Deskford and Cullen, Baron Strathspey

Was born at Edinburgh on 7th October, 1851, he served as an officer with the 1st Life Guards. He was exceptionally well loved by his tenants and clansfolk, and it came as a great shock to the whole of Strathspey when, after a brief illness, he died at the early age of 33. Unmarried, he was succeeded by his uncle:

26. JAMES OGILVIE-GRANT
9th Earl of Seafield

He succeeded in 1884, but lived for only a very short time and was succeeded by his son:

27. JAMES OGILVIE-GRANT
10th Earl of Seafield

There is quite a romance to this Chief. As a very young man, and before his father became Earl, he worked his passage as a sailor 'before the mast' to New Zealand. Here he was variously employed as a carpenter, house-painter, and general odd-job man. It is said that he was actually painting a house when word was brought to him that he had succeeded to the Earldom. Unfortunately, he did not long enjoy his elevation, dying in 1888.

With four Chiefs dying thus within a space of seven years the great Seafield Estates were imperilled by Death Duties, and the Dowager Countess Caroline, widow of the 7th Earl, showed considerable business acumen by placing the estates in the hands of trustees, with an entail which prevented succeeding heirs assuming full title until they had reached the age of 40. The wisdom of this was proved when:

28. JAMES OGILVIE-GRANT
11th Earl of Seafield

Was killed in action in France, November 1915, in his 36th year. As he had never held full ownership of his patrimony the estates were not liable for death dues. His Scottish honours and estates passed to his only child, Nina, the present Countess of Seafield, who took over control of her estates from the trustees in 1948. The Chiefship of the Clan, however, passed to the 11th Earl's younger brother:

29. TREVOR OGILVIE-GRANT OF GRANT
6th Baron Strathspey

Was born at Oamaru, New Zealand, 2nd March, 1879, and resided at Rottingdean, Sussex. He married Alice Louisa Hardy-Johnstone, of Christchurch, New Zealand, by whom he had one son and one daughter. He was succeeded in 1951 by his son:

30. PATRICK DONALD TREVOR OGILVIE-GRANT
OF GRANT
7th Baron Strathspey

He was born in March, 1912, and is the present Chief of Clan Grant. The line of succession followed here is mainly in accordance with *Grant's History of Grant*. This places the present holder 30th in the line from Gregor, but the pedigree recognized by the Freuchie Grants themselves designates him as 32nd Chief of the Clan.

CADET FAMILIES OF GRANT

1. GRANTS OF GLENMORISTON
(Clan MacPhadruig)
Descended from Ian Mor, natural son of John, 10th Chief of Grant.
OFFSHOOTS
1st Grants of Ballindalloch and their cadet families.

2. 1st GRANTS OF BALLINDALIOCH
Descended from Patrick, second son of Sir Duncan, 9th Chief of Grant.
OFFSHOOTS
Grants of Advie
Grants of Ballintomb
Grants of Carron
Grants of Dalvey
Grants of Dunlugas
Grants of Rothiemay
Grants of Tomvoulin
Grants of Tulloch

3. GRANTS OF ROTHIEMURCHUS
(Clan Patrick)
Descended from Patrick, 2nd son of John, 14th Chief of Grant.
OFFSHOOTS
2nd Grants of Ballindalloch
Grants of Tulliegrew
Grants of Corrower
Grants of Kinrara

4. 1st GRANTS OF WESTER ELCHIES
Descended from James Grant, who obtained the lands in 1541.

5. 2nd GRANTS OF WESTER ELCHIES
Descended from Patrick, 2nd son of James, 18th Chief of Grant.

6. GRANTS OF EASTER ELCHIES
(Clan Duncan)
Descended from Duncan, 2nd son of James, 13th Chief of Grant.

7. GRANTS OF GARTINBEG
(Clan Connachie)
Descended from John MacConnachie Grant, who died 1553.

8. GRANTS OF CARRON
Descended from Ian Roy, natural son of Ian Mor of Glenmoriston.

9. GRANTS OF TULLOCHGORM
Descended from Patrick, 2nd son of Sir John, 8th Chief of Grant.

10. GRANTS OF CORRIEMONY
(Clan Ian)
Descended from John, 2nd son of John the Red Poet, 12th Chief of Grant.

OFFSHOOTS
Grants of Urquhuart
Grants of Sheuglie

11. GRANTS OF MONYMUSK
(Clan Gillespie)
Descended from Archibald, 4th son of James, 13th Chief of Grant.

OFFSHOOTS
Grants of Ardnilly
Grants of Tombreck

12. GRANTS OF KINCHIRDY
(Clan Mungo)
Descended from Mungo, 7th son of John, 17th Chief of Grant.

OFFSHOOTS
Grants of Gartinbeg
Grants of Knockando
Grants of Tomdow
Grants of Tulloch-gribban

13. GRANTS OF BALMACAAN
(Clan Thomas)
Descended from Thomas, 8th son of John, 17th Chief of Grant.

OFFSHOOTS
Grants of Achnastank
Grants of Culvoulin
Grants of Ballifurth

14. GRANTS OF LURG
(Clan Robert)
Descended from Robert, 3rd son of Duncan, 15th Chief of Grant.

M

15. GRANTS OF GARTINBEG (See No. 7)

OFFSHOOTS

Grants of Kinveachy
Grants of Dalrachnie
Grants of Inverlaidnan

TRADITIONAL BRANCHES

16. GRANTS OF BURNSIDE
(Clan Chiaran)

Descended from Lucas, 3rd son of Gregor, 1st Chief of Grant.

17. GRANTS OF AUCHERNACH
(Clan Alanach)

Descended from Alan, 4th son of Gregor, 1st Chief of Grant.

PRONUNCIATION OF "AVON"

The proper Gaelic spelling of the loch, strath and river called
Avon ' is *Abhainn*. Many years ago, when surveyors and carto-
graphers were getting out their very excellent Ordnance Map, an
attempt was made to simplify the pronunciation of some Gaelic
place-names by rendering them into phonetic English. In this instance, however, there was an unlooked-for trap.

Generally speaking, the combination of the letters *bh* in Gaelic is
used to convey the sounds of V or W, there being no such letters
in the Gaelic alphabet. The map-makers knew this, and thought,
therefore, that they were being helpful in replacing *bh* by the letter
V in *Abhainn* and rendering it phonetically as ' Avon '. What they
did not know, unfortunately, is that *bh* is also used in Gaelic to
separate similar vowels, and when this is done the *bh* becomes silent.

Thus, the proper phonetic spelling is ' A'on ', and it should never
be pronounced in any other way, even though, like its Brythonic
counterpart ' Avon ', it simply means ' River '.

NOTE ON FAUNA

I cannot say for certain when a full assessment was last made of the fauna of Strathspey, but I do know how misleading it is to place any faith in the lists tendered by writers of fifty years ago.

Dr. Forsyth, for instance, in his very excellent book published in 1900, begins his review of the various species to be found here with the definite statement: "Sixty years ago the *Wildcat* was not uncommon. It is now extinct." Then, two paragraphs later, he adds: "Sixty years ago the *Woodpecker* might be heard at work in the forest. . . . Nothing now remains to tell of its history but the oval-shaped holes, which may be found in some of the older trees."

All that may have been accurate enough in the Rev. Doctor's time, but it is far from true to-day. I saw a Wildcat as recently as 1946—with a rabbit in its mouth, it was entering a hole in the steep larch-bank of the Spey at Polchraine—and never a summer goes past without me both hearing and seeing a Barred Woodpecker in the Crow Wood at Cromdale. This bird, by the way, is noted as a rare vagrant in Scotland, seldom detected north of Manchester.

And so it is also with other animals, such as the Badger and the Hedgehog, so scarce in Dr. Forsyth's day that they were classified "probably extinct". The Badger is now as prolific here as anywhere, with the Hedgehog possibly more so. I should say that the only animal definitely known to be extinct within the past four hundred years is the Wolf; the last survivor of this species in Britain having been killed in practically every district of the Highlands. In Strathspey, the honour of thus finally exterminating the scourge is granted to *Sorcha Mor* (Big Sally), a Duthil woman, who is reputed to have performed the deed with a gridiron.

Owing to the lack of gamekeepers during the war years the Fox population increased tremendously, with a consequent lowering in the numbers of game-birds, but Fox drive-shoots within the past five years have now reduced this threat to less serious proportions. In the winter of 1948-49 the tally of foxes shot in our district of the strath was 104, and when it is remembered that the Mountain Fox is a very much bigger, and more voracious, creature than his brother in the lowlands, it will be realized what a fillip this gave to the rearing of Red Grouse, Pheasants and other game.

Otters are still plentiful, and in the winter of 1952 one was killed by a car while crossing the road on Dava Moor. It was a grand specimen, measuring more than four feet in length and, in the words of the car-driver, " as fat as butter ".

The Red Squirrel, surely one of the most charming denizens of our woodlands, is still with us in large numbers, but in 1954, on the fringe of the Mid Port plantation, I saw, for the first time in this area, a Grey Squirrel. This was a disturbing discovery, because experience in England has shown that where this hybrid rodent becomes fully established, extinction of the harmless and decorative red variety invariably follows. I informed the local keepers of this menace, and I myself now keep a weather eye open when I go out with a gun.

The Crested Tit, for so long noted by naturalists as exclusive to Strathspey, has recently been found in certain restricted areas of the North-west Highlands; but without bringing any noticeable lessening of their numbers in their original habitat. Some Ospreys have also been seen in the Highlands west of Strathspey, and there is growing hope that a pair of these may find their way back to the ruins of the castle in Loch-an-Eilean, where they previously made their home for so long.[1]

Pleasing visitors to Cromdale in 1953 were a flock of Greylag Geese. A skein of these touched down in the glebe land behind the manse at the beginning of the winter, and remained for many weeks. Unfortunately for themselves, they varied their stay here with two fleeting visits to the Moray Firth area, and this resulted in a slight depletion of their number. On their first arrival here there were eleven all told; when they departed there were only nine. Perhaps some sportsman along the sand-flats at Findhorn could tell us where the missing two went.

Strathspey is particularly rich in bird life, and many of the varieties common here (Ptarmigan, Snow-buntings, Crossbills, etc.) are not so readily met with in other parts of Britain. One has only to read a book like Desmond Thompson's *Greenshank* to appreciate what an engrossing pastime bird-watching can be in this locality.

During the lovely summer of 1947 I came upon a pair of Pied Flycatchers nesting by a stream within fifty yards of my dwelling. As these birds generally breed in the west of England and Wales, and are only very occasional visitors to the South of Scotland, I thought at first that I might be mistaken as to their identity, but a letter from a correspondent to the *Sunday Times* proved that I

---

[1] *LATE NOTE:* The ospreys have returned to Strathspey. They are nesting in Glencoe. During 1955-56 they have been seen fishing in waters as far apart as Loch-an-Uaine and Loch-an-Dorb.

was not the only person to note their presence in the Highlands. These birds, or their offspring, returned to the same nesting site three summers running. They may still be doing so. I moved my place of residence in 1950, and so have had no opportunity of proving up on the point.

I have a very old game-book which records the wide range of beasts and birds that have fallen to my rifle or gun in various parts of the world. The entry for Strathspey notes the following:

Roe-deer, Fox, Stoat, Brown Hare, Mountain Hare, Rabbit, Caper-caillie Black-cock, Grey-hen, Red Grouse, Pheasant, Snipe, Mallard, Pintail Duck, and Teal. Although only a very small fraction of the wild life to be found here, this makes quite a little list of fauna in itself. I should add, however, that all these creatures have been shot either for the pot or as vermin, and never from any sheer joy in killing.

Although practically exterminated by myxomatosis, the once ubiquitous rabbit is still fighting a grim battle for survival. During the winter of 1955-56 a widely distributed number of rabbit tracks have been noted in the snow all over the strath. These suggest that one more 'extinct' species may again become prolific in the years to come.

FROM A BIRD-WATCHING DIARY

The following birds have been seen in Strathspey by the author between the years 1945-1953:

Bittern
Blackbird
Black-cock
Brambling
Bullfinch
Bunting, Cirl
     „   Corn
     „   Snow
Capercaillie
Chaffinch
Corncrake
Crossbill
Crow
Cuckoo
Curlew
Dabchick
Dipper
Dotterel
Duck, Eider
     „   Goosander
     „   Mallard
     „   Pintail
     „   Sheld
     „   Shoveller
     „   Teal
     „   Widgeon
Dunlin
Eagle (Golden)
Fieldfare
Fire-crested Wren
Flycatcher, Pied
     „   Spotted
Geese, Canada
     „   Greylag
     „   Pink-footed
Goldcrest
Goldfinch
Greenfinch

Greenshank
Grey-hen
Grouse, Red
Gull, River
     „   Common
Hawfinch
Hen Harrier
Hedge Sparrow
Heron
Hooded Crow
Jackdaw
Kestrel
Kingfisher
Kite
Knot
Landrail
Lark, Meadow
     „   Wood
Linnet
Magpie
Marten, House
     „   Sand
Moorhen
Owl, Barn
     „   Long-eared
     „   Tawny
Oyster Catcher
Partridge
Peewit
Peregrine Falcon
Pheasant
Pipit
Ptarmigan
Raven
Redshank
Redstart
Robin
Rook

Sandpiper
Siskin
Snipe
Sparrowhawk
Starling
Stonechat
Swallow
Swan, Common
     „   Mute
Thrush, Song
     „   Mistle
Tit, Blue
     „   Cole
     „   Crested
     „   Great
     „   Long-tailed
     „   Marsh
Tree-creeper
Twite
Wagtail, Grey
     „   Pied
     „   Yellow
Warbler, Garden
     „   Grasshopper
     „   Reed
     „   Sedge
     „   Willow
     „   Wood
Water-rail
Waxwing
Whimbrel
Whinchat
Woodcock
Woodpecker (Barred)
Wren (Common)
Yellowhammer

BIBLIOGRAPHY

History of Moray (3 vols.) by Lachlan Shaw.
The Chiefs of Grant (3 vols.) by Sir William Fraser.
Memoirs of a Highland Lady by Elizabeth Grant of Rothiemurchus.
Letters from the Mountains by Mrs. Grant of Laggan.
In the Shadow of Cairngorm by Dr. W. Forsyth.
The Cairngorm Hills of Scotland by Seton Gordon.
Vacation Notes in Strathspey by Arthur Mitchell.
Greenshank by Desmond N. Thompson.
The Secret of Spey by Wendy Wood.
My Scottish Youth by Sir R. Bruce Lockhart.
The History of Clan Shaw by Norman Shaw.
Tales of Moray by Sir Thomas Dick Lauder.
Lochandhu by Sir Thomas Dick Lauder.
Primitive Beliefs in North-East Scotland by J. M. MacPherson.
MS. Account of the Rise of the Name and Offspring of Grant by
    Rev. James Chapman.
Old Statistical Account of Scotland.
Survey of the Province of Moray.
In the Steps of the Clansmen by James Alan Rennie.

INDEX

INDEX